WITH OR WITHOUT ME

Esther Maria Magnis

TRANSLATED BY ALTA L. PRICE

WITH OR WITHOUT ME

A Memoir of Losing and Finding

Plough

Published by Plough Publishing House
Walden, New York
Robertsbridge, England
Elsmore, Australia
www.plough.com

Plough produces books, a quarterly magazine, and Plough.com to encourage people and help them put their faith into action. We believe Jesus can transform the world and that his teachings and example apply to all aspects of life. At the same time, we seek common ground with all people regardless of creed.

Plough is the publishing house of the Bruderhof, an international community of families and singles seeking to follow Jesus together. Members of the Bruderhof are committed to a way of radical discipleship in the spirit of the Sermon on the Mount. Inspired by the first church in Jerusalem (Acts 2 and 4), they renounce private property and share everything in common in a life of nonviolence, justice, and service to neighbors near and far. To learn more about the Bruderhof's faith, history, and daily life, see Bruderhof.com. (Views expressed by Plough authors are their own and do not necessarily reflect the position of the Bruderhof.)

ISBN: 978-1-63608-026-0
26 25 24 23 22 1 2 3 4 5 6 7 8

Front cover image by Sanjeri/iStock.com. Author photo by Hank Visscher.

Originally published under the German title *Gott braucht dich nicht.*

A catalog record for this book is available from the British Library.
Library of Congress Cataloging-in-Publication Data

Names: Magnis, Esther Maria, author. | Price, Alta L., translator.
Title: With or without me : a memoir of losing and finding / Esther Maria Magnis ; translated by Alta L. Price.
Other titles: Gott braucht dich nicht. English
Description: Walden, New York : Plough Publishing House, 2022. | Summary: "Where is God when your loved ones get cancer? With or Without Me is an unsparing and eloquent critique of religion. Yet Esther Maria Magnis's frustration is merely the beginning of a tortuous journey toward faith. Esther Maria Magnis knows believing in God is anything but easy, because he allows people to suffer"-- Provided by publisher.
Identifiers: LCCN 2021043191 (print) | LCCN 2021043192 (ebook) | ISBN 9781636080260 (paperback) | ISBN 9781636080277 (ebook)
Subjects: LCSH: Magnis, Esther Maria. | Christian biography--Germany.
Classification: LCC BR1725.M216 A3 2022 (print) | LCC BR1725.M216 (ebook) | DDC 274.3/083092 [B]--dc23/eng/20211020
LC record available at https://lccn.loc.gov/2021043191
LC ebook record available at https://lccn.loc.gov/2021043192

Printed in the United States of America

"The Nothing is spreading," groaned the first. "It's growing and growing, there's more of it every day, if it's possible to speak of more nothing. All the others fled from Howling Forest in time, but we didn't want to leave our home. The Nothing caught us in our sleep and this is what it did to us."

"Is it very painful?" Atreyu asked.

"No," said the second bark troll, the one with the hole in his chest. "You don't feel a thing. There's just something missing. And once it gets hold of you, something more is missing every day. Soon there won't be anything left of us."

— Michael Ende, *The Neverending Story*

RED

1

1

A thorn had scratched my leg. It was from a blackberry bush. I had spotted three red dots in a field of yellow grain, and immediately sent my bike's silver handlebars, whose pink plastic grips gave me blisters because they were too small for my hands, swerving toward the side of the road. I had hopped off, letting my bike fall into the grass, and jumped over a little ditch. I'd heard a ripping noise – a thorn had torn a red gash into my leg, and a thin line of blood emerged. It wasn't much, just enough to turn the cut bright red without oozing out any farther to run down my leg.

I didn't care. Because there were the poppies, within reach. I wanted them. The wind was barely audible, the day and the fields were dozing in the sun, and the flowers' delicate petals fluttered as I yanked their roots from the soil, squashed their stems between my hands and the handlebars, and rode home. One leaf was lost on the way, and another as I pulled up to the door. And then, in the vase that evening, the blossoms drooped and the petals fell to the table. I tried this over and over as a kid. I'd always pluck another poppy, and was always a little disappointed when it wouldn't bloom as bright or as red in our kitchen.

Behind my closed eyes it was also red. From there, it was easy to sink into sleep. It was dark, too, but not dangerous; I knew this darkness, and found it comforting. Only when someone turned on the light, or I tried to sleep at the beach – then it was too bright. Otherwise, I liked the red behind my eyelids.

I had a calendar with nature photography where I discovered a red frog amid bright green leaves. I couldn't believe it was real. I asked Mom, and she said it was, and that nature is full of amazing colors. She read me the photo caption from the calendar, and told me about the crabs in Africa whose red carapaces looked like caravans of little tanks crossing the road, back when she met my father.

I just can't imagine large red things in nature. I can picture bloodbaths, when whales with white bellies swim up to the surface, but I don't really want to call that nature. Maybe it is nature, I don't know. It depends on how you perceive human beings and the things they do.

The first thing my little brother and I asked to do was pet the puppies. Our babysitter's parents had a farm, and two weeks before, their dog had had a litter in their green-tiled spare bathroom. Once we heard about it, we begged her every day for permission to see the newborn pups.

It stank in that bathroom, I bumped my head on the sink, all the little creatures were crawling about, and I asked if I could take one home with me, but the babysitter disregarded my question. Apparently I was supposed to ask my mother or father first.

Right next to the bathroom was a kitchen, and a bunch of old men sat on benches in the nook. There was a huge yellow ashtray on the table, like in a pub. The kitchen was filled with smoke. The men laughed as our babysitter walked us past the doorway. "Kids suit you," one of the old grandpas said.

"Cut it, Dad," the girl said, and I was astounded that the man with so few teeth left could be her father. I was four years old, and somehow I'd already grown fond of Westphalian farmers, despite being creeped out by their huge, chapped, red hands, which always crushed the fingers of anyone they greeted.

I had a tic: I couldn't help clearing my throat whenever they spoke their Low German dialect, because to me their rolled r's made them sound like their throats were blocked with phlegm.

"We're just going to visit the piglets, and then I'll take the kids home," our chubby babysitter said.

"Atta girl," said one of the men on the bench.

The piglets were in a crate right behind the kitchen, in a dark little passageway. One wall of the crate was just a bunch of nailed-in planks, so at first you could only hear a muffled, high-pitched snorting and a light bumping sound against wood and a shuffling of straw on stone. The only light came from a red lamp in the crate, and you could see the little snouts poking out of the slits between the planks.

Johannes held my hand. The babysitter walked with us, right up close to the crate, and I peeked through one of the slits.

The red light made my eyes feel too hot to look, or maybe the piglets' skin was too warm. In any case, it felt like a layer of something was coating my gaze, and nothing looked as real as I might have hoped. But my little-kid heart melted when I saw the pinkish-red creatures and how they wriggled excitedly, wagging their wormlike tails.

I just wanted to pick them up and kiss their little wet snouts and pet them and rock them in my hand and lather them with pink shampoo and hug them close. I wanted to bring them home and put them in my baby doll stroller so they'd never grow up.

"Can I have one, please?" I asked, exactly as I had before, with the puppies.

The babysitter laughed. "One of the piglets? Forget about it, kid."

"But you have so many! You could give just one to me and Johannes. Right, Johannes? You want a piglet too, don't you?"

My little brother beamed and nodded. He always thought my ideas were good.

"You can't need all of them, so you can give one away to us," I said, and stuck my arm far into the crate, sleeve rolled up high, so I could pet as many as possible, all at the same time. Johannes pushed up next to me and thrust his arm along mine and patted around, pawing at the piglets I would have preferred to have to myself.

"But what are you going to do with all of them?" I asked the babysitter.

"Well, they'll be raised for slaughter," she replied, and I felt my mouth form the "slaugh-" and the "-ter" as I tried to silently echo what she'd said; both syllables felt brutal but also grown-up. In any case, I sensed it was a word adults might be annoyed at being asked about. So I didn't ask. I couldn't have, anyway, because in the meantime Johannes had peed his pants and the babysitter had taken him to the bathroom. I wanted to stay with the piglets, so I was left all alone in the room, which as a kid gave me a strange sensation that was at the same time exciting and oppressive.

I can't remember how long I stayed there, nor what I actually did during that time. But I remember the squeal.

It sounded like someone had thrust a jaggedly sliced tin can into the mouth of a screaming woman. It rattled from the windpipe, through the nose, groaning, arising from the belly and suddenly growing shrill, reaching the highest, airiest pitch.

It pierced the hallway door, a towering, dark double door directly opposite the kitchen door. This was the door Johannes and the babysitter had vanished behind and, as my initial fright subsided, it was the door I had to go up to. I was afraid of annoying the adults. It was just like with the word "slaughter," which I didn't dare ask about, because it clearly wasn't anything for a little kid, but this time I simply *had* to go and see.

As I stood on my tiptoes in order to reach the iron doorknob, I was more afraid of being caught than of seeing something scary. What kind of scary thing could I have dreamed up, anyway? I had no pictures. I wasn't allowed to watch the news, hardly watched TV; I'd only been in this world a mere four years. But somehow even little kids can sniff it in the air when something's up, and I just had to see for myself, even if only by peeping through the crack of the door.

As I bent forward on tiptoe and leaned against the door, it swung open slowly, heavily, yet unstoppably, crashing against the hallway wall. I stood in the doorframe and could smell blood steaming up from a kind of tub. Above it hung a sow, slashed open, and I wondered whether that was what had squealed. Her feet were bound by a noose hanging from a huge hook, and the men were pulling red stuff from her belly.

My memory is filled by a red haze; in some spots it's as dark as the red behind my closed eyelids. The men wore aprons – they were towering figures. They were incredibly focused, and I just stood there and stared and kept staring, the way you stare at a math problem you're supposed to be able to solve.

"Somebody get the little one outta here," yelled one of the men in a blood-covered apron. He had a knife in his hand. I wasn't afraid of him. For me, he was the epitome of a grown-up: a massive, serious, busy stranger.

The door was shut again, and through the slit I heard someone shout, "Anni! Dammit, Anni, keep an eye on the brats!"

Anni came back, holding Johannes's hand, and drove us home. I wasn't traumatized. I was fed meat as a child. Sausage and a slice of bread. *Kinderwurst,* a fun-shaped baloney, at the butcher. I had no choice, no way of opting out. Just like my baptism. In both cases, nobody asked me. The first thing I drank was milk. Then came pureed vegetables and, with my first teeth, meat.

From the very beginning, I went along with it.

2

"Vain," someone whispered. "You're a vain one, all right."

As I turned around, I clenched my hair tie between my teeth. Both hands were at the back of my head, holding up my ponytail. My hair had gotten mussed up during playtime. I just wanted to quickly straighten it out again, and now I found myself staring at an old woman's face.

She held one child by her right hand, another by her left, and they were standing behind me at the entrance to church. She said: "God doesn't care about superficial things like your beautiful hair. Here's how it's done." She let go of the children's hands and bowed her head. She bore a blue-haired perm under a hat that looked like a homemade knit purple tea cozy. Then she clasped her hands together, and looked back at me.

"Not like this," she said, rolling her eyes and patting her hair with a few gestures that I supposed were meant to signify vanity, and repeating, "Oh, my hair – aren't I so cute?" Then she thrust a hand into her purse, dug out a handkerchief, quickly wiped her mouth, put it back in her purse, and just as speedily took the children's hands back into hers. Usually kids were allowed to go to catechism on their own, but she pulled them along with her, passing all the rest of us to go up to the benches at the very front.

This woman was a deputy in the classroom where children were prepared for their first communion. I never had to deal with her after that, but I was afraid she might be a direct deputy of God.

I just wanted to look put together while entering church. I didn't want my ponytail to be hanging askew, starting just behind my right ear and then flopping forward all by itself, while the hair on the other half of my head danced in the air like haunted spaghetti after my wool pullover had given it a static charge.

I was the only child who didn't become an altar server after celebrating first communion. I didn't want to. "I do *not* want to serve the priest," I told my mother.

"You are not serving the priest, you're serving God," she had replied, but at the time, that had struck me as an excuse. The entire Mass centered on the priest. He stood behind his altar just like my teachers stood behind their lecterns, and we had to kneel in front of him.

It was similar with confession. I was actually excited at the prospect of taking a seat in the confessional, until I found out that we first communicants had to have the initial conversation directly with the priest, because someone had decided the confession box was too impersonal. Maybe. I'm not sure. Maybe our church just didn't have a confessional. But people told me the same things about confession that they had told me about altar service – namely, that you weren't confessing your sins to the priest, but to God. But now, talking face-to-face with the priest, it sure didn't feel like that. The night before my first communion I lay in bed and hoped and prayed that I would find God the next morning in church. We first communicants had to stand in a half-circle around the altar, facing the congregation. Everyone looked at us. A host was placed into our hands, and on the count of three (once the priest was back at the altar) we had to place it into our mouths. Something about it made me feel ashamed. As I chewed, I looked at my feet.

All in all, my parents were fairly understanding of us kids when we were bored by church. I even got the general impression that most people found church somewhat less perfect than they'd have liked. When I was growing up, in the eighties, there was just something in the air – a sense that something was unfinished. That some goal hadn't yet been reached.

I'd heard it said that too little was being done for the youth.

Sometimes during Mass a band at our church would play catchy tunes like "Laudato sí" and a song urging us to plant a tree that would give us shade, and build a house that would protect us, or something like that. I didn't really understand it, but I did my best to warble along, tapping my feet to the beat as the drum and flute stumbled through the stanzas. Moments like that weren't boring, which was good. But I never would have voluntarily gone to Mass just to hear the band, that's for sure. It was just something for the kids who had to sit there anyways.

The real revolt in our household occurred when my parents tried taking us to an ecumenical service for a second time. As soon as she heard the word, my sister Steffi protested loudly, and I whispered something about "ecumenical bullshit." My mother was angry.

"Your father and I have an ecumenical marriage. There are countries where Protestants and Catholics are at war. I don't ever want to hear anything like that from you again."

"Ecumenical." I repeated the word quietly, rolling my eyes.

"You're so mean to us!" Steffi groaned. "Please don't make us go. The last ecumenical service went on for ten hours. It was awful. Can't we *please* just stay home?" At some point my parents finally took pity on us, gave in, and left us at home.

In fact, the first such service we'd gone to had lasted two hours. First the Protestant pastor had blathered on about how great ecumenism is, and then, just as everyone had sighed with relief as he left the pulpit, up came the Catholic priest and repeated the same thing: "It's good that we're here," and all that stuff. Yeah, everybody thought it was great that we were all there. Everybody but us kids. Nobody stood up, except during the Our Father and the Apostles' Creed, which the choir recited sluggishly. A few of the Protestants stumbled at the spot where they say, "I believe in the holy Christian church," instead of "I believe in the holy catholic church." There was no standing, no kneeling, no nothing, really – everyone was basically glued to their pews. For hours. It's etched into my memory as a form of physical torture.

We usually went to Catholic Mass on Sundays, but we'd also gone to a Protestant church fairly often, since my father was Protestant.

Even as a child, I remember noticing how much freer and lighter my parents would sometimes seem, plopping back into the car when a church service was over. I'll never forget how my mother once cheered out loud as we got home. She popped an old black-and-white movie into the VHS player, sat back in her leather lounge chair, propped her feet up, and said, "Well, my dears, sometimes it's just so nice to have done something, isn't it?"

Actually, I liked God. I often found him boring in church, but aside from that I found him fundamentally intriguing. There seemed to be something insane about him, and also something gentle.

He was clearly fond of John, who ran around the desert half-naked like some exhibitionist, covered only partially by camel hide, yelling his lungs out and munching on locusts. And he seemed to like that revoltingly crazy possessed man, who was totally out of his mind. He even spoke with the devil. He gave orders to the sea. And he bled on the cross – from his head and his back, and he was covered in filth and welts. He seemed pretty wild.

But then, at other times, I got the feeling that he wore glasses, knotted his hair into a bun, had a long beard, and stared dead ahead, empty-eyed. I had once heard a pastor say that God didn't like it when kids went out to play soccer on Sundays instead of going to Mass. I found this thought deeply distressing. It wasn't like the Sunday soccer matches had been organized by us eight-year-olds. They were scheduled by the coaches and a few of the parents, and as kids we were supposed to listen to them, weren't we? I found that pretty ignorant on God's part. Sort of stuffy. Or more like grumpy. But then those moments passed. I squirreled them away in my memory, but they didn't override my interest in him or my attention. Because as a kid I mostly just found him extraordinarily beautiful. And extraordinarily friendly. And weird.

There was a moment – I was still quite little, maybe five or six – when I was all of a sudden absolutely certain that he existed. I think the gratitude I felt for the sheer beauty of that moment bound me to him for a long time.

It was one night in Spain, on the Atlantic coast. I was alone, on a promenade. My parents and siblings were in the restaurant behind the sea wall lining the beach. My father was a businessman whose international trade work frequently took him around the globe. He often brought us – the whole family – along. We kids sometimes had to be there for his meetings, and get along with his coworkers' kids. We were always polite and attentive. We would teach each other how to say things like *table, napkin, waiter, knife, fork, spoon, fish, shrimp,* and *ice cream* in one another's language. I always liked the smell of the Spanish girls' hair – it struck me as festive. That evening the client was a good friend of my father's. I already knew his two sons – they were much older than I was, and already absorbed in the adults' conversation, in English. Steffi and Johannes were still spooning their ice cream out of coconut half shells. I didn't want any. I was bored.

"Don't go too far, Estherle," my father had said to me as I stood at his side, stroking my fingers on his tie and asking if I could leave the table. "Nope, I won't. I'll be just outside."

The other businessman looked at me the way foreigners look at kids speaking German with their parents – quizzically, bemused – and then said something nice about me to my father, in English. I already knew. I grinned, a little embarrassed but also flattered by the attention. He winked at me. I tried to wink back, but couldn't.

As I stood at the table, the ocean suddenly came to mind. It had been right behind that wall the whole time. I wanted to go and see what it was like all by itself, without beachgoers, by night. I slipped through the narrow aisle between the tables, past the glass-door freezer full of gigantic gawking fish on top of crushed ice, and through the restaurant's swinging doors. Out into the orange glow of the streetlights. Then I turned the corner and headed onto the promenade, and there, black and vast, lay the sea. The promenade was actually a boardwalk, about three yards above the wide beach. The surrounding terrain was full of large sandstone rocks rising up from the dark sand below. I could smell it. I went a little farther, just beyond the streetlights' reach.

I stood before the infinite sea, with no endpoint anywhere between the left and right corners of my eyes. That's how far the beach stretched. I walked over to the rocks, which came up to my bellybutton, climbed onto one, and sat down with my legs dangling over the edge. The rock was warm. Muted strains of music from the restaurant reached my ears. Spanish music, and voices of people who go to dinner around ten thirty at the earliest.

I could only barely make out the hazy shape of the waves in the darkness, but I heard the sound of their breath as they heavily exhaled onto the shore about a hundred yards away, rolled themselves over the sand, and then sharply drew air back in through pursed lips. That's what it sounded like. There were no lights, just the moon on the water, shining from far behind me. I hummed along with the sound of the waves, and looked out across the broad beach all the way to the narrow strip in the distance, where the gleam of the water ended and the dark of the sky began. The cosmos. I don't know whether I already knew that word. While I was watching, the depth of the heavens – something you glean when you stare at the stars – began to grow right in front of me. It was a sensation I'd never known; it was utterly new to me. The sound of the waves didn't soften, but seemed to take another direction. Their whoosh was no longer toward me, to my little place on top of the rock, but rather outward into the distance. The rocks and the sea, the glimmer on the water's surface, the stars and everything behind me – all of this lay at the feet of what was bearing down from the new depth of sky.

I felt like an unnoticed part of this whole, and found it beautiful. I waited, and watched, though I had no idea what was actually happening.

Inside of me, without consonants, without vowels: my name.

The world wasn't stepping back, but I was stepping forward, out of it. Out from the night, because my name was echoing within me. The entire time. And with certainty, though without me saying it.

It had a gravity that was loving and at the same time absolute, unconditional. Not the way an adult might look at a child. And in its lingering gaze there was something indescribable, something heartening, that gave me the feeling I had to take myself seriously. A knowledge of myself that I couldn't fathom. Encouraging and at the same time approving, authorizing. I was so astonished that I have no idea how long I sat there. And then all of a sudden I was pretty sure, and burst out: "You're God?" Thinking: "That's God? That's what adults mean when they talk about him?" And because I found his devotion and affection so touching, I raised my hand from the warm rock and gave him a little wave. And because I felt so grateful, I decided to give him a little gift. I stood up on the rock and composed a prayer.

I rest, I dream, I go to sleep,
dear God, protect me and keep me
always in your hands . . .

And then I faltered, because I didn't know how to put it. ". . . Keep me always in your hands, so that I can find the way. The right way. I must find the right way." I strolled along the beach, then stopped and looked out to sea again, my gaze returning to the horizon. But the only glistening I saw was the moonlight. The waves whooshed onto the beach. God was gone. It was a letdown, and I couldn't understand. "Well, he could've stayed a little longer," I thought.

"Steffi?" I whispered that night, right after we'd gone to bed. She hadn't fallen asleep yet. Mom had just turned the light out and left the room.

"Steffi?"

"Yeah?"

"God is super nice."

She was quiet for a bit.

"How's that?"

"He thinks I'm good. You too, probably. He's super nice."

"Yeah," she whispered back, "I think so too."

All my childhood prayers rhymed. As I entered adolescence, they were mainly a bunch of blather. Well, not entirely. Before every math, chemistry, physics, Latin, French, or English exam I prayed with the intensity of a beggar. If I got an A, I cheered. "Awesome, thanks!" If I got a C, I was silent, with that awful feeling many people know – the feeling you get when you've prayed and rustled up the necessary faith only to find yourself facing the opposite of what you'd asked for. At times like that I either thought, "Well, you didn't study hard enough. That's what you get. God wants you to give it your best, and a blow like this should make you smarter." Or, "What? Damn it."

It was at this age, around thirteen or fourteen, that I slowly began growing apart from God. It was simply a separation. No waving, no goodbyes.

It was as if we were at the airport, standing on one of those moving walkways. We were looking at each other, and then we were carried off in opposite directions. Without a word.

The more sermons I heard, the more I got the feeling that I could no longer live and act according to his expectations – and that we no longer had that much in common.

This feeling was only exacerbated by the crazy claims and excessive expectations of some sermons. Some struck me as the recitations of tightrope walkers, so high and lofty, set in such a politically charged world, going on about Africa and foreign relations, that as a teen I thought: I can't do anything about all that. God doesn't need me. It's not that I was shrugging my shoulders. It was just utter helplessness. And it was supported by generalizations and commonplace phrases that I found nutty, and that I eventually grew sick and tired of. Someone would say, "We mustn't look away, we must get involved." And I'd think: How long do I have to gawk at the TV, how long am I supposed to stare at the pictures in the newspaper, before nobody can accuse me of looking away? And just how am I supposed to get involved?

The same phrases could be heard both inside and outside the church. I don't know who was trying to outdo whom. I remember once in school, we were supposed to protest the Gulf War, and "get involved." I didn't. I went home and asked Dad where Iraq was, and what was going on there. They'd neglected to cover that in school.

In church, depending on the priest and the sermon, God seemed to be someone who wanted the world to take on a specific shape. Listening to one priest, I got the feeling that the kingdom of heaven would dawn only if and when everything went back to being as it was in his youth in the Harz mountains, in the seventies. Listening to another priest – or was it a pastor in the Protestant church? – I got the feeling that God's will seemed to be, mostly, that the conservative Christian Democratic Union be voted out. Still another railed against greed. Even that struck me as stupid. Not in itself. It was more that every time I'd sit through Mass, watching the congregational leader nod, I'd wonder, "If everyone here thinks the same about everything already, why do they all have to come back here every Sunday to have it fed to them again?"

The feeling I was grappling with was not humility. Humility is a wonderful feeling. You can be humbled by things that are larger and more beautiful than you, things you gladly fall silent before, things you're happy merely to be in the presence of.

This wasn't humility. All the things that God apparently wanted from me were impossible. After all, it's not as if I had Chancellor Kohl's telephone number.

And I held it against the church. I took offense at the idea that I was supposed to be like your typical eco-activist high school teacher, or like a buttoned-down kid from back in the seventies who giggles at phrases like "making out" and who thinks singing "Kumbaya" around youth-group campfires is super-rebellious.

My encounter with God hadn't been that. I still had no idea what he wanted, but I was interested in him; somehow something bound me to him. His divineness. His reality. But a lot of what I'd heard about him had turned him into a stuck-up moralizer who, just for fun, had come up with the idea that people should go to church every Sunday. Why? No idea! It's just what you do. More and more, my relationship to God began to resemble a worn-out, rubbery old piece of chewing gum that had been chomped on for too long.

I knew you should love your neighbor. I also knew the question: "But who is our neighbor, dear congregation? Who is our neighbor? It is the outcast, the beggar, the leper, the prostitute . . ."

But I hadn't, not even once in my entire life, seen a prostitute. A beggar, sure, but not in my hometown. And leprosy? I didn't know anyone who had that. Such neighbors seemed far away indeed. That might be practical for people who are accustomed to the idea that God doesn't have anything to do with their daily lives. But for me, as a teenager, it wasn't. I hoped and intuited that God belonged to this world here. I wanted him to like me, because I liked him, because I found him important. But, in all honesty, somehow, by the age of fourteen, I had also come to understand that it's good to be nice to my actual neighbors as well. To my classmates and friends when they're struggling; to comfort and help them, if I could. I really didn't need to go to church every Sunday to be reminded of that.

And since everything I heard said in such sermons could also be heard on all the talk shows and everywhere else – sometimes in different words, but usually the same formulations – the notion that maybe going to Sunday Mass was utterly superfluous began sneaking into my mind, little by little. The world had enough morals. They were constantly flung at us, from all directions. That we should show consideration to minorities and take care of the weak, and that politicians are bad people. For that, you didn't really need to go to Mass – the young atheists in my class were right about that. "You can be a perfectly good person without believing in God." True. Just like you could also be an annoying moralizer without going to church.

On TV you could watch women with heavy blue eye shadow and enormous earrings jangling next to hair that was long on one side and undercut on the other, yelling at each about how "this system is wrecking the earth, humans are the destroyers, down with TetraPak!" And you could go to a sermon and hear exactly the same thing.

And so I was often astonished at how such huge swaths of society went out of their way to draw a line between themselves and the church. I found that there was just one tiny step separating the Christians I knew from everyone else. They all wanted to save the environment. They all wanted to be tolerant toward other religions, though also to see a little less of the pope. They all wanted church to be a little more relaxed; it all came back to our common "humanity," and so on. Even the images hanging in the showcases in the lobby of our little church looked exactly like the ones from UNESCO and similar organizations: a big globe ringed by children of all different skin colors holding hands, nice and colorful. Images like that were popular everywhere back then.

"Paint peace." That's how I painted it. "Portray love." That's how I painted it. "Today we'll explore reconciliation." That's how I painted it. It worked out great, as long as the teachers were always different and as long as we were asked to paint, not to debate. I muddled my way through these pictures in various classes and always got an A. By then I knew that no teacher could possibly resist an image like that: they presumed it portrayed what we kids yearned for. Whereas I presumed it portrayed what my teacher yearned for. Final grade: A. Thanks.

The only thing that made the church different from society at large, as I saw it then, was that the church believed that Jesus was very important. But even there, the more that Catholic and Protestant descriptions of him swirled around in my head, the more I lost interest.

I had plenty of other friends. As a fourteen-year-old, I really didn't need another – certainly not an invisible one, much less one who looked like a Middle Eastern pacifist in sandals and a long beard who, I figured, couldn't possibly take much of an interest in me, since I was neither a prostitute nor a tax collector. Plus, we had a Mercedes I was sure wouldn't fit through the eye of a needle. The more low-threshold the version of Jesus was that we were being offered, the less my friends and I could relate to him. You might as well just file him right next to Gandhi under the category "guys who were all right."

And when I heard the general intercessions during Mass, provided I could understand them – they were often recited by children who couldn't really read yet, or had a heavy lisp, or were unable to decipher words like

"Chechnya," or were simply too short to reach the mic – I increasingly noted that even the church itself didn't really have much confidence in Jesus.

"Lord, in your goodness: many are ailing; send people to their bedsides, who will bring them a comforting word." I wasn't totally stupid back then. I knew that this intercession, fully formulated, went on like this: "We're not asking you to do the impossible. Since you usually don't do much of anything, and so as not to wear out the stories of miracles performed by Jesus, maybe you could just send some nice people to the bedsides of the sick. It's pretty much a request you can't refuse, and no one will accuse us of spreading hope where there is none – we're just holding down the fort. You need us. Because we can do something, and you can't."

I remember one of the grotesque songs we had to sing. It went something like this: "God needs your arms, because he has none. He needs your hands, so he can take action. Tra-la-la, shoo-be-shoo-be-doo, oh yeah." It made sense to me at the time; at least it was totally reasonable to think like that. But God grew increasingly smaller. And I was more and more astounded that the world and the church couldn't stand one another. When it came to believing, the bar really wasn't so high anymore.

There was just one point that I could have identified back then on which the church and the world took starkly different positions: guilt and sin. Take the word "sin." People hated it, or found it laughable. Before my first communion, as I prepared for my first confession, some of my friends' parents even made fun of the idea: "What sort of evil can such a young child have committed?" the mother of one of my girlfriends wondered. I solemnly nodded, while remembering, for a second, the frog I'd once tried to squeeze into a toy car even though it was obviously too tight a fit; and the little girl my sister and I had once dangled out of the attic window, just because we knew she'd wail and then we could console her and take care of her like a real mother would.

Or guilt: people were always sensitive about that. I'd heard it said that guilt was what was used to control the masses during the Middle Ages. And before the Middle Ages people were especially afraid, because it was "so dark," as we'd all learned from Ken Follett. So people accused the church of playing games with guilt.

Meanwhile I heard it said on TV and in school that people are influenced by their environment, and that there is actually no such thing as guilt, in and of itself. That people had invented the idea in order to fill the confessionals. "How hypocritical of the church," I'd heard. And sometimes I thought, "how hypocritical," too.

The real problem, of course, was bad genes and bad childhoods. Or so people said. And the fact that old-fashioned notions of guilt were still in circulation, and that people were still looking for scapegoats – well, there again, people said, the church was actually the guilty party.

But church and society were of one mind above all regarding their chief concern: correct behavior. The church's opinions were always explained and justified by interpretations of the word of Jesus. Those of society – I don't know – by values, which were around here somewhere, since someone had written them down once. I lost my sense of what God wanted of me in life, beyond traffic laws and all other basic laws, social action, and a heart and soul that aren't totally screwed up. Sometimes I still prayed to God. I held still, and listened.

Sometimes I sat in my little pink room, alone on my bed. Next door, Dad was napping; Mom was down in the kitchen. I could hear pots clattering, and Steffi on the phone, and my thoughts would turn into a prayer. It would stem from these sounds, it would resonate. It was rare, but sometimes the world even seemed to come to a halt, to turn off for a moment, and an unbridled, perfect, consummate "yes" would express its agreement, even though I wasn't doing or saying anything. I was just sitting on my bed. A plain and simple yes. But if I'm honest, no matter how nice I found that to be, in the long run, it was too little. Because God didn't want sanctimonious prayers, he wanted actions, as I had learned.

This attitude infected my faith.

3

Empty plates lay in front of us.

"Children . . ." Dad didn't look at us – if he did, it was only for a second, so as to keep his gaze from meeting ours and dragging us down into the abyss opening up just behind his eyes. It was midday, and we were seated at a round table in the room next to the living room, which was all decked out for Christmas. I was fifteen.

The oldest furniture in the whole house was in this room. It even still had an old hatch in the wall, for the dumbwaiter that connected the former kitchen and the cellar. The world outside was as quiet as always on Christmas Day, when everyone stays indoors with their families. I sat on the other side of the table, with my back to the bay where a bunch of black-and-white pictures of my great-uncles and great-aunts hung on the wall, as well as big round paintings of my great-grandmother smiling next to her husband and my somewhat sterner looking great-great-grandparents. To my left sat Johannes, near the curtained entryway to the living room. Steffi sat to my right. Mom had set a tureen of soup on the table, then silently sat down next to Dad. He looked almost bug-eyed.

"Children . . ." Another three seconds passed. "We have something really, really – we have something . . ." and then his voice choked, his eyes teared up, and we stared at him, scared. Dad never cried.

Mom took Dad's hand without looking up, and held it tight. We were frozen with fear, and I stared at the parting on her bowed head, a white line between her black hair. Finally she spoke, in a quiet voice. "We have something very sad to tell you." Dad's sobs interrupted her, but then he got ahold of himself. I couldn't breathe – it seemed as though a nightmare were taking shape, growing in toward us, from every direction, and then the walls dissipated, leaving just the five of us, seated at the round table, suspended in darkness. As quickly as it had appeared, the nightmare could have retreated – the walls, floor, and ceiling could have returned and the room gone back to being a room. But then Dad said he was going to die soon. He said the doctor had given them bad news. He had cancer, it was untreatable, and nothing more could be done.

My sister let out a soft shriek. She didn't cry, but her voice was so high that it seemed to be coming from her nose, if not from between her eyes. "Then what did he say? What did the doctor say?"

"Three weeks, maybe three months," Dad said, and from twenty yards away – no, even farther, from far, far off – I heard my sister crying – no, whimpering – and my brother, equally far away, cried, and Dad too – and inside me a stone rose from the pit of my stomach into my throat, the stone that had just been punched into my stomach, as if I weren't a girl but a guy with a knife whom you had to punch like that, as if I didn't have a soft belly and would never have gotten into a fistfight, as if I were a trained fighter who would recover from a blow like that in a few of days, as if it wouldn't tear me apart, as if the fist were mistaken and had hit the wrong person, since surely no one could ever have meant to punch a child so hard they'd puke.

"But I don't believe it," the stone in my throat banged out, and my eyes spat out a few tears, and I took another breath. My body had to recover. It was like it had suddenly fallen asleep, like a cramped foot, with no circulation.

All around me everyone was crying and sobbing. Mom, Steffi, Dad, Johannes – each like a kid from a different family, unknown to one another, as if someone had thrust them all together, naked, in the same room, with the door locked, and each had responded with their own special form of fear. Like kids unable to comfort one another. The empty porcelain plates shone bright white. I'd gotten one that didn't have any pink petals painted on it.

He'd fight for us, Dad said, his head between his hands, and then he looked straight up at me, his face all red and wet with tears, his nose dripping, his teeth clenched, and one hand balled up in a fist. "I'll fight this damn cancer," and he nearly spit out the word "fight." "I promise you, I swear, I'll do anything to stay here with you," he said, and as he did so, he looked at me as if he were tearfully asking my forgiveness.

Dad's father had died when he was seventeen. He knew far better than we kids the horror he'd be fighting against for us.

4

My memory only picks up again a week or so later. Up in the mountains. I'm hiking, looking down at my boots. I can't remember any further back than that. The snow crunches under my feet, a bitter-cold wind is blowing, and the crisp, glittering crystals sting as they strike my face.

I smell the scarf covering my nose. It smells of the wardrobe it lives in all year when I'm not wearing it of Dad's winter hat and after-shave, of Mom's leather gloves, of my brother's hair, our dog, and my sister. We're away from home. We've driven seven hours, out to our cabin in the Black Forest – my grandmother's home.

And now we're way up in the meadows. Surrounded by nothing but pastures, lying pristine and fallow, high above the villages in the valley below. Not a soul in sight. Small snowflakes whirl over the mountain ridge, and my mind is empty. I have a snapshot, taken when we reached the summit – Mom, Dad, Steffi, Johannes, and me. Who took it? I have no idea. Even then, my mind was devoid of all thought. Maybe someone just set the camera's timer. I hear the phrase "the last family portrait" in my head, and then it's all silent again. The wind blows incessantly, whistling, and you can't talk because it's so cold, and for a second you're astonished it's so blindingly bright even though you can't see the sun and it's cloudy all around, and the only spots without clouds are all snowy. White mountains, white sky. We walk by three ancient, gnarled trees I've known since I was little. They're bent, as if buffeted by a gale. One side has hardly any branches, and on the other the branches look as if they're being sucked in by some invisible force. Like women with wind at their backs, parting their hair on the back of their heads, blowing it forward so it flutters horizontally around their faces.

Somewhere up there, I notice it. Somewhere up there, while I'm walking and staring at my boots and the snow, I notice that something inside me is thinking of God. And has been for a long time already – the entire time. Except that my mind is empty.

5

I wake up. My eyes open to a green-white blur. I'm looking at a tapestry. I'm in bed in the children's room, in the cabin, I think. And then it comes to me: "I want to keep Dad."

I stay in bed for a bit because I'm not yet fully awake, and the lingering fog of heavy sleep still needs to clear from my head and limbs before I can get up. Steffi's in the bed against the opposite wall. It's so cold I can see my breath. Whenever we're here, we sleep in the attic room – the children's room, where my uncles slept when they were kids.

I stick my arm out from under the thick duvet and try to turn on the smelly space heater. As I touch the knob, I think: "I want to keep Dad."

I grab for the wool socks near the bed, and pull them on under the covers. I get up, drape a blanket over my pajamas, and hold it wrapped around me with one hand as my other hand turns the doorknob. "I want to keep Dad," I think, quietly – as quietly as I open the door in order not to wake Steffi. Brushing my teeth, as I gaze into the mirror, I know it, quite calmly: I want to keep Dad. I spit the toothpaste into the white sink, rinse out my mouth, and go down the stairs. The steps creak, and I open the door to the living room and – there he is, seated at the table, the sun glistening in his hair. The sentence evaporates from my head.

I walk over to him, he opens his arms, and we hug. "Morning," I mumble into his sweater. "Morning, Estherle," he says. I sit down across from him.

And as I bring the mug of hot chocolate to my lips, and am about to take a sip, I can't, and I set it back down. I want to keep Dad. I stare at my plate. I want to keep him, but I don't tell him that, because he needs to be free to fight. He needs every ounce of strength at his disposal.

It went on like this for days. As I squinted into the sun, and as I spread my bread, I wanted to keep Dad. When I lay in bed at night, smelling the space heater and listening to the babbling brook in front of the house, and my sister whispering, "Sleep tight, Esther," every fiber of my being merely responded, "*I want to keep Dad.*" The sentence sprouted from behind my brow; it took root in my heart, blossomed in my belly, tugged at my toes, grew from my fingernails, extended from each strand of my hair, and lay in every drop of sweat upon my skin. Periodically, I could even feel that sentence in my throat as I breathed. I only really noticed when it had taken shape and was almost complete, when it had swollen and made me feel jittery. Then I'd let it move as it liked. It twirled slowly, like a large, unfurled sail. I left it alone and let it have its way. And when it stopped moving, I thought: "God," and was aligned.

That's what's so easy and graceful about youth – the way it can still just let things take it and go with it.

This prayer or mantra or whatever you want to call this thing that had sprung up within me was different from every other turning toward God that I'd had up to that point.

I was the prayer. Entirely. Every bit of me wanted my father to survive. And it wasn't like usual, with prayerful thoughts carefully woven into acts. I didn't censure myself the way I usually did.

When I had fallen for some boy and wanted him to like me back, I would agree with God that if the boy didn't have a crush on me, maybe he was the wrong one. I would readily admit that God probably knew better than I, but "please, nevertheless, hopefullys\.s\.s\.well, it'd just be so nice, if you want . . .I mean, personally, I'd be really pleased if . . .I just like him so much, dear God; please make him like me back. Thy will be done, but please, please, make him kiss me."

In cases like that, I wanted something, and then I'd think of something, and then some kind of humanistic, western European, nineteen-nineties-type morality would kick in, and my head and my heart and my gut – the instincts we hold in such high esteem, which we're ostensibly supposed to heed – would bat it around. And then I'd turn the desire over, inspecting it, asking myself whether it was a good one, and whether it was good for me, or good to even have. Then I'd ask myself if God might have the same desire or plan in store for me. And then I'd realize that I actually couldn't care less, that I didn't give a damn if God had some other plan, because he really got on my nerves with all his other plans, the kind you could only guess at, or had to cobble together from the Bible. And yet, I simultaneously believed he nevertheless existed, and had something to do with my life, and so I prayed – bearing all these tangled thoughts in mind, but never really knowing what to expect, or what criteria might apply, or what anything going on in my life had to do with him, if anything actually was going on . . .

The question that remains is why anyone prays at all anymore. After all, you can be polite to God just by going to church on Sunday, by bowing to the tabernacle.

All this thinking and feeling, all this wondering what God is like, and what he might want, and what I want, and what I might hope for – all that was gone after I'd gotten the news and absorbed the message, and after my prayer made itself felt within me. The sheer shock of it had bulldozed all my thoughts. The adult notion of warding things off with reason was unknown to me. The voice that might suggest, "Be reasonable now, don't indulge any false illusions – miracles might happen, and you can even pray for them, but don't forget that your dog was put to sleep despite your prayers to the contrary, and that your neighbor died despite his piety. Sure, maybe there is a God, but to believe in divine intervention is just wishful thinking. Most people can handle a little rough stuff without having to clutch at straws. Let's first try rising to the occasion. Let's first try chemo . . ."

At fifteen there aren't so many *ands, ifs,* and *buts.* They're there, but with any luck they imply flexible questions doing an odd kind of dance, rather than doubts etched in stone.

So I didn't really think about it much. I noticed that a subtle urge began to exert itself in me, here and there. I just let it happen. It got bigger. Then my thoughts said, "I want to pray," and my heart said, "Yeah, me, too," and my gut said, "I was about to say the same thing," and my tongue said, "I'll go ask Steffi and Johannes if they'd like to pray with me," and then my sense of logic butted in and said, "Nah, not yet. I'll stay on the lookout for the right moment."

It came a few days later, one evening in the kitchen, once every part of me had finally come to agreement.

And so, right there in my Grandma's old kitchen, as my siblings and I washed the dishes after dinner, I said, "I want to pray." My sister momentarily broke off rinsing and said, "Yeah, me, too," and my brother said, "I was just going to say the same thing." That was it. It had been spreading in them, in the same way it had in me, and turning them in the same direction.

"Where?" Steffi asked. "Up in the attic?"

6

The iron doorknob was cold as ice, and the entire attic was as chilly as the snow cloaking the roof. In the dark you could make out the contours of chests and wardrobes in which old white bodices, long underwear, and baby bonnets still lay wrapped up in yellowed newspapers from the 1920s. The air was so cold and fresh – whatever dust was covering the floor and furniture lay undisturbed. But you could still faintly smell it.

We tried to be quiet. We didn't want the adults to hear us. It had been ages since I'd last done this – softly tiptoeing, feeling my way across the floorboards, feeling through my wool socks for the places that wouldn't creak.

None of the adults knew what we were up to. We hadn't told them – not Mom, not Grandma, not our aunts nor our uncles. It was too personal, too intimate. And as we snuck across the uneven floorboards, I worried that one of them might come and ask what we were up to, or just walk in and discover us praying in the dark – which would have been really embarrassing. Probably all three of us would've been ashamed. We planned to pray for a miracle, even though we'd been taught to interpret the stories of Jesus' miracles in such a way that none of them seemed to have much of anything miraculous left. Jesus couldn't walk on water, it had been a sandbank. Jesus hadn't made the blind see, he'd just taken the "blinders" from their eyes so they could see the misery of others – that of their neighbors, for example. Jesus hadn't raised Lazarus from the dead, he'd just drawn him out of his "isolation and his self-imposed social deadness" and brought him back into the "community."

A few years ago, a little deacon explained to me why, when praying for intercession, you couldn't ask for the sick to be healed – for miracles. If you do, he clarified, the congregation would immediately have a theodicy problem on its hands. "Oh, I see," I replied with a hushed voice, looking around anxiously. "You mean your flock still hasn't heard that God doesn't necessarily heal everyone who's sick?" And then I leaned toward him and whispered into his ear, "I won't tell anyone. I promise. Let's let sleeping dogs lie – or sleeping sheep." He didn't find it funny.

Johannes flipped the old black light switch, trying to turn on the dim sheet-metal lamp dangling above the attic ladder, but it was broken. So we just proceeded in the dark, sneaking up to the little room that was our destination.

None of us had any preconceived notion of what should happen next. I wasn't one to dash off quick prayers. In this case, my prayer was perfectly ripe. It had matured over the course of a few days, deep within me. But now that I needed to express it, I realized I hadn't yet found the right way. None of us had. Steffi quietly and carefully closed the door behind us. We bowed our heads under the slanted roof. Downstairs everyone was watching TV, or playing backgammon, or trying to cope with the absurdity of how every second of Dad's life now held weight. It was all unbearably heavy. It almost made you impulsively jump up and suggest that everybody start dancing, or do something grand and beautiful, even though everything is as heavy as a convict's last meal.

We stood in the little attic and hesitated. A dim, blueish light shone through the triangular window, faintly reflecting off the snow-capped mountain now shrouded in night across the valley from our cabin. Against the wall, in the dark, was a wooden bed. The duvet covering it formed thick, high mounds. As Johannes went to sit down, the duvet puffed up to his right and left. He sank down into it and sat there, in the trough of what looked like a little origami boat with steep sides.

Steffi and I pulled two stools over to the bed. It was cold. For maybe thirty seconds, we didn't say a word. Then, in the dark, I made the sign of the cross and began mumbling, "In the name of the Father," and my siblings quietly chimed in, "of the Son, and of the Holy Spirit. Amen." Silence again. We got that far. We still knew that much.

More silence.

I had the urge to pray, but I didn't know what to say or how. I didn't want to hear my voice. I figured it would never be able to adequately express what I felt – that the belief in my heart would never manage to will itself into shape between my tongue and gums. I was afraid my voice would just be left hanging in the air. It was a fear I'll bet many people know, kind of like when you want to say, "I love you," and you really mean it, but it comes out so clumsily – foolishly lingering there in space, unworthy of being believed, parroting itself – that it's embarrassing. I was afraid that once my prayer was voiced, I'd have to watch it break apart and fall to the floor like crumbs, or dissipate in mid-air. And once that happened, I'd no longer be living between bad news and a prayer, but be left facing nothing but uncertain terror.

More silence. It contained our collective waiting, perhaps for one of us to just begin saying something. But these moments passed. It was too serious to just start talking. One of our stomachs made a noise. I pondered what I wanted to say. My siblings did the same. But we all stayed silent. Tense. Waiting. No one spoke.

We had never sat together like this. But we got through it – those minutes when people might let out a sigh, or cross one leg over the other, or fidget like people do in church or at concerts. We stayed silent. For minutes on end.

And then our silence suddenly grew still, and out of it came a tugging. It wasn't my siblings waiting for me to speak. They weren't waiting for me, and nor was I waiting for them. No. In that silence, a calm emerged. A peaceful patience. It was not our waiting anymore. It was *His.*

The peace of mind that filled this patience wasn't one we ourselves could feel. This peacefulness wasn't ours, but we knew that it was the truth. And truth always only poses one question. And the only answer is "Yes," and it utters itself. All we could do was nod along with it, adding our own words.

Steffi whispered, "You said that when two or three people gather in your name, then you are among them. That's what you said. And there are three of us here, Jesus. Please make Dad healthy again."

And Johannes: "Please perform a miracle, dear God. We haven't always gone to church, and I haven't prayed much. But you can perform miracles."

And I: "*Please* perform a miracle. Please make Dad

healthy again. Please don't let him die. We believe in you."

God. Larger than back on that seashore in Spain. As clear as "I am." Clearer. Surer, more certain than you or I or anyone.

I often think of that prayer when I find myself speaking with acquaintances who don't believe in God, but know that I'm a believer. So often they'll concede, "Well, sure, I can easily imagine that prayer is calming, or feels good. It's probably very comforting if you believe someone's always there."

I keep quiet, because I know I can't reasonably expect someone who doesn't believe to suddenly trust what I have to say about the reality of God, the reality we kids experienced back in that attic. We'd experienced the same reality – all three of us. And we knew as much right afterward. But I can't explain that to these acquaintances, nor would I ever tell them this story. Because then they might be the ones to keep quiet, out of pity or shame. Over the fact that me and my poor siblings were in such distress back then that our psyches conjured it all up. A hallucinatory bout of wishful thinking induced by our group dynamic.

For a long while afterward, my siblings and I didn't talk about the episode up in the attic. But from then on, whenever God came up in general conversation, I noticed that they were talking about the same God as I.

We never articulated it. At most, we'd say, "You know what I mean? Like that time up in the attic, when we prayed?"

We knew. We understood without ever having to explain it to one another. The following week, we prayed together like that every night.

7

The air was warm and humid and thick with the yeasty scent of pizza dough and beer. The pub's low-hanging lamps cast orange spheres of light over each table, and anyone who leaned too far back in his chair ended up vanishing into the black just beyond. So I only saw Dad every now and then, when he'd lean in, his face taking on a yellowish glow. He was sitting at the head of the table, at the far end from me. Johannes was on my left, and Steffi straight across from us. One or two girl cousins and a boy cousin – I can't really remember – plus a few aunts and uncles were also there. Everyone was trying to focus on the meal, despite the news that Dad's cancer was terminal – trying to just eat the pizza. Two days had passed since we had prayed together in the attic, or maybe three or four. From time to time, under the table, I'd take Johannes's hand in mine, and he'd smile at me. Steffi looked at me every now and then, her eyes inquiring, "How are you doing? How are you feeling now?" and a half hour later I looked at Johannes with this same question in my eyes, and each of us kept answering the others with a smile, a sign of hope. It was real hope. A little astonishing, but nevertheless real. It said "Yes."

Everyone drank a lot of wine. They always did, and their eyes were already glassy, their cheeks red, and many were even laughing. My father appeared less and less frequently in the lamplight. More and more I could see only his hands at the edge of the table, folding a napkin, or stroking the tablecloth, fingers laced together, one hand kneading the other, unfolding the napkin, stroking the tablecloth. One of my cousins told a joke and we laughed – I laughed, too – but I kept sneaking a glance back over at Dad to see if his face had reappeared in the lamplight, so I could read it, or something like that. After my cousin's joke, other family members told a few more – that's just how our family has always been, and still is. And then Dad was suddenly popping up out of the darkness, leaning in, and looking over at us. He was gazing up at us, his head slightly reclined, his hands resting on the edge of the table, propping the rest of him up, and his eyes straining, longingly. His mouth was restrained – lips pressed tight, as if he were all torn up inside but trying to keep the pain bottled up, at bay. His deep eyes flickered in their sockets, and everything about his posture made it look like he was about to duck down, or was already cowering. The cancer stare. I hadn't recognized it until that moment. And I didn't know yet that it could get even more dreadful, even more intense. Dad leaned over toward my uncle – Mom's brother – and said something. I looked back toward the people on my end of the table, and then away again – I didn't want everyone to notice me staring – and then turned to gawk at Dad. When I glanced back in his direction, he'd already stood up, disappeared into the darkness, and was opening the pub's front door. It closed behind him, the sound muffled by its padded frame. My eyes met my uncle's, both of us anxious and uncertain. "Let me through," I said to Johannes, sliding my foot behind his hands on the bench. He leaned forward, and I held on to his shoulders as I squeezed up and over behind him. The table grew quiet. Mom said something. I pushed on the pleather door handle and strode out through the thick, waxed-canvas entry curtain. Outside, the ice-cold air froze my nostrils. There was snow on the ground, the kind that lingers after a storm and looks like the ice lining a freezer in need of defrosting. It was almost New Year's Eve. Down the pub's outer wall a bit, toward the unlit street corner, I saw my father. He looked baffled, inconsolable, deathly afraid. He was staring at the ground, and I got the sense that he was trying to hold himself together, since he kept combing through his hair with his right hand, sucking in his breath through clenched teeth, and then tossing his head backward and looking straight up at the sky. That's when he saw me.

I went up to him and slid my hands into his. I felt stupid – but I also felt bad for him; he seemed so helpless. "Dad," I said softly.

He briefly pressed his closed eyes with his thumbs and pointers, and let out a groan. Then he took my face in his hand, fingertips on my cheek.

"Estherle," he exclaimed, his voice cracking. "It's just . . . I was actually so happy in there with you kids, I just . . .I couldn't – Shit! It's just such a mess."

He pulled me closer. He was holding himself together, but it was a strain. It took effort; I noticed it from the way he held me.

"Hm, hmm." I quietly hummed, and took his hand in mine. He relaxed a little. "Did I scare you, Estherle? You don't need to be afraid, girl," and he kissed the top of my head.

"Dear God," I thought. I sensed how vulnerable Dad was at my side, and I held his hand, and wanted to give him something of what I believed, what I knew. And that's the first time I felt a nervousness I often feel to this day. I thought: He needs to pray. All this won't do a thing. He needs to pray, that's the only way. He should speak to God. Soon. But how could I tell him? It's not like I could say "Pray, my brother in the Lord, and you shall receive help."

"I love you, Dad." That was all I could manage.

"I love you too."

Then we went back inside.

8

"Shit." I'm sitting at the table in the living room of my grandmother's house. My younger cousin is sitting across from me. There's a backgammon board between us. I made the first move, sliding the thick white chip forward, and now it's Grandma's turn. She rolls the dice, thinks it over, and in the few seconds of silence while she's calmly inspecting the board, I all of a sudden think, "Shit." My heart is racing. I raise my hands to rub my face. "Shit. I'm scared. Oh God. Shit! Shit! Shit! I'm scared. Don't do it! Don't do it. Leave him with us. God!"

I slide back and forth on the bench; I can barely stay seated. "Your turn," my cousin Leah says, and her doe eyes peer out at me from her little-kid face, drilling deep into mine. I act as if I'm pondering my next move, leaning my forehead against my hand. "You have to roll first," she reminds me. I roll. I move my chip. I actually want to run upstairs to Dad, but I stay put. Then I breathe a little more deeply and slowly, and think that this can't be self-sustaining, this belief. Belief-wise, I'm obviously not sitting in some kind of secure boat floating downstream on some wide, gentle river. No. I'm going to have to make a more proactive decision. In favor of God, maybe. I don't know. I don't even know what God expects of me, aside from prayer. Does he want me to start going to church regularly now? I'll do whatever you want, God.

It doesn't matter what; I'll do it. I'll work the streets, if you want. Just tell me what to do! He says nothing.

That evening, back in the living room, I quietly say to Johannes, "Should we head upstairs?" He stands and goes with me toward the door, where Steffi's already waiting for us. Dad suddenly turns to us from his chair. "What are you guys doing up there all the time, anyway?" he asks.

He rises and comes over. He's staring at us. To actually tell someone you're praying for them can leave an after-taste, like arrogance. It's like saying, "I'm looking after you." And to say something like that to a charismatic, strong-willed person – especially when that person happens to be your own father – well, it seems a little crazy.

Johannes looks at his feet. "We pray," he says.

"What are you praying for?" Dad asks, and in his voice I can already hear that he's ready to let a little piece of his strong, fatherly role fall by the wayside, and make room for something else.

"That you'll live," I say quietly. I'm unable to look at him. Instead, I'm staring at the carpeted floor, my socks, Dad's corduroy pants, Johannes's socks, and then Dad's sweater as he hugs me, and Steffi, and Johannes – all three of us at once. He pulls our heads together against his chest and his voice breaks, as he lets out a single astonished word: "You!"

Johannes's forehead presses against Dad's sweater, tears streaming down his face, his mouth shut tight, his eyes closed – I see it all from close up. Steffi's nose presses against the back of my head. I feel her light, steady, warm breath in my hair and on my scalp.

"Can I come with you, if you're going up now?" Dad asks, and slowly lets go of us.

We kids go upstairs in front of our parents, up to the cold attic, and as I open the door at the top, I wonder just how this is going to work. What if God doesn't show up? What if Mom and Dad look at us while we're praying and find us sweet – what if they think it's a touching sight, but don't really pray along with us? As I climb I realize that I have no idea whether Dad has ever really spoken to God from the bottom of his heart before, or if he's always just recited prayers, kind of like the way he's always just worn a suit to the office. I really hope God comes into the room with us again. In my head I whisper: make Dad see you and believe in you. And Mom too.

Because we wanted to be on the safe side, we decided to pray precisely the way we'd done it the first time up in the attic. Steffi began with her classic rendition of "When two or three people gather in your name," and I added the same thing I'd said that first night. I don't know what my siblings had in mind, but I guess that they felt the same way I did – just hoping against hope that God would come to us, and therefore using the same formula, and praying with so much feeling that it would just have to be like that first night. So that God *would* come.

As it turned out, the first few minutes were a bit off. But then things loosened up a bit. Dad prayed. He thanked God for our family. He cried. We kids cried, too, but not out of fear. We cried because we believed that this way – all of us seated before God, the whole family in prayer – a miracle might really happen.

9

"There's someone lying in the sauna. With his clothes on. I don't know if he's dead or what, but you better get him out." My sister was standing in my bedroom door, looking super upset. Still in bed, I turned over and propped myself up a little. Oh God, my head. I was so hung over I could barely lift it.

"Mom and Dad will be home in a couple of hours, and they shouldn't have to deal with this mess. Dad's doing really bad, Esther. We need to clean up the house and get rid of those guys."

I could hardly think. "Dad's always doing really bad," I managed, lamely. Steffi walked off.

Dad's first round of chemo had worked. That much had affirmed the calm trust we kids had had in God ever since the first time we prayed together up in the attic. But then his cancer had come roaring back, snarling even more loudly than before. Louder and fouler. Mom and Dad did everything they could. He'd kept his promise: he'd fought with all he had. They'd flown to the United States, gone all over Germany, made calls as far away as Jerusalem. They'd bought teas from African herbalists. While we kids were home alone, more and more often.

I wanted to just roll over again and go back to sleep, so that my head would stop pounding. But then I thought about Dad, and pictured him sitting in the car, in terrible pain, as he and Mom drove home from yet another hospital somewhere – who knows where? The very idea made me angry, and it made me get up, go out to the sauna, turn it off, and open the door. It was scorching hot and smelled beyond gross. There was a beer bottle standing in the wooden sauna bucket, and a guy passed out on one of the benches. Fully clothed, socks and all. He had pulled one arm out of his sweatshirt. His face was bright red, his mouth hanging open. I could tell he was still breathing mostly because of the stench. I tried to shake him awake.

"You gotta go, now – my parents will be back soon."

On my way through the basement laundry room I spotted a pile of unfamiliar clothes on the floor in front of the dryer, and – peering through the dryer door – a dime bag of whatever drug it was that dumb couple who had shown up last night had tossed into it. I reached in and extracted it. My parents hated drugs. Dad hated them so much, he wouldn't even let the doctors give him morphine. Instead, he listened to Bach fugues. He'd lie out in the sunroom, while I'd secretly stand or sit behind the door and listen to the music – a strict beat and high notes which the pianist sometimes hummed along with, I guess because he couldn't help it. Sometimes I'd hear Dad moaning and hope that this strange, disciplined musical straitjacket could somehow catch his pain, harness it, and hold it under control. I remember hoping that the music could somehow train or direct his pain, and diminish it. Dad didn't know how often I secretly listened in, nor did he know that I sometimes sat behind the door, disappointed, pressing my face into my arm and letting my tears soak my sleeve when the music suddenly stopped right in the middle and it became clear that Bach had lost the battle, and that Dad was in such pain, he had punched the mantelpiece with his fist.

Temples throbbing, I picked up the pile of clothes and staggered up the basement stairs. Two people were lying on the floor in our hearth room. Naked. On the stone floor.

"Dude," said Johannes as he appeared in the other doorway, still sleepy-headed and wearing only his boxers. He was gaping at the couple and grinning. "Who's that?"

"No idea," I replied, "But they have nice asses."

We laughed, which woke them up, and I quickly flung the clothes over their butts as they started stirring and stretching.

The phone rang. Johannes took it. "Hm-hmm. Okay," he said, "Yeah. Nah, we just partied a little." I could tell it was Mom. "Hm-hmm, I will. Yes. See you soon."

He came back into the room. "We got an hour. Ugh, uhh . . ." He rubbed his face, ran both hands through his hair, and scratched his head. "Dad's not doing so well. You get rid of everyone, and I'll take care of the empty bottles, okay?" I nodded.

We rarely went to the hospital with them, so we were on our own more often now. But we hardly prayed together anymore. We'd grown tired after so many months of ups and downs, talk of cancer progression and news of rising marker levels. Our prayers had been reduced to single sentences we each uttered privately, by ourselves: "Please make Dad healthy again." And at the same time I knew this prayer had direction, and I had hope, even when I wasn't really conscious of it. When an illness drags on for so long, first growing horribly acute, but then dozing off again for a bit or slowing to a creep, at some point such a prayer begins to feel and sound a lot like any other – "Give us this day our daily bread." Well, we had bread. And pork roast and dessert, too, and Dad had lived another year and a half so far. Meanwhile, the doctor's previous prognosis now seemed completely overblown. I just couldn't take the disease so seriously every day – I couldn't pray for his life on a daily basis. It was the same for all of us. Especially when Dad was doing well, it seemed hysterical and overly dramatic, praying for him to survive.

Should you work yourself into a state of panic in order to be able to pray more earnestly or truthfully? I didn't. I only prayed when the news was bad. But even I couldn't say the phrase "Please make Dad healthy again" anymore. I just couldn't stand hearing myself say it.

That morning I was so hung over that I lurched through the house, hating that I had to rush around cleaning up, hating not being able to just be a teenager thinking teenage thoughts. "This is bull. If the parents freak out, who even cares . . ." I was so worked up that day that I even talked to God as I knelt in front of the fireplace and wiped up puddles of spilled beer: "Cure Dad already. Do *something!* Look, we got it: we know how precious life is. Really, we understand. We all love each other. What more do you want?"

I wrung the rag out into the bucket, slapped it back down on the tiles in front of me. "Nah – that's all wrong. Forgive me, Lord. I'm just tired. Please make Dad healthy again. *Please.* I'm just so tired. I do believe in you. But we're waiting for you."

I put all the bottles into bags and sent the drunks home. They said their goodbyes, cracked a few last jokes, and then disappeared. I finished tidying up. I prepared the house so it could hold more suffering and shuddering. I prepared it so the miracle we were all waiting for could finally happen.

10

Neither of us spoke. The hallway carpeting muffled our footsteps, as well as every other sound. Side by side, Steffi and I walked through the huge, white doors – extra wide, to accommodate heavy hospital beds and gurneys – and approached the elevator. As Steffi pushed the button and we waited, she looked my way with a smile. Then sweetly and softly asked me, "Well?"

I didn't say anything. I just smiled back. Our appearances had changed lately. We looked more tired. More serious. Mom in particular. And Johannes, the youngest. Sometimes it looked as if there was an ancient, black lake behind his eyes. I couldn't have said where it was, but I was certain we'd never played there together. Sometimes an impatient wrath flickered within me. Against God. Because my brother had grown so silent. Because I no longer knew how he was doing, even though I had always been so close to him.

Dad had begun a new therapy, and it required in-patient hospital treatment. There were flowers on the heavy bedside cart, and his after-shave bottle, next to the disinfectant dispenser. Outside the window, the sun was setting, and there were huge, blood-red clouds whose ruddy glow gave way to broad swaths of increasingly black ones.

Mom stayed there, and was given a room next to Dad's. The hospital was far from home, and he was getting worse.

My brother and I had moved to a boarding school nearby. Steffi was staying home alone, since she was in the middle of her college entrance exams. At boarding school Johannes and I prayed together, but only very rarely, off in a corner of some hallway or in my room.

We had just returned from a silent retreat at a monastery – where we had neither reflected nor kept silent – when the father of one of my boarding-school girlfriends died of cancer. This friend and I bought a bottle of vodka, and then walked out to a waterfall and sat down in the snow next to it. There she calmly told me about her father's death. She talked on and on. With each sentence I took a gulp of vodka and patted her like a madwoman, my desperate fear propelling my hand ever faster. But it was fine; she didn't stop me.

Afterward, I ran to Johannes and told him we had to pray for Dad. He looked back at me from those wide, fearful eyes and softly said, "Okay," and we prayed. Our prayer took us on a journey into darkness, just like when we played adventurous games as kids, except that this was an entirely unfamiliar darkness. This time, we couldn't imagine what the enemy looked like, and we had no campfire, no weapons, no sticks to use as swords to protect ourselves. All we had were words – his voice, my voice – surrounded by desks and chairs, the light of his desk lamp, a bird chirping outside, the church bell chiming the time, and the school bell ringing. Everything seemed innocuous, resonating in the harmless, warm, bright, but wooden tones of school furniture and rec lounges. All seemed peaceful, despite the fact that this was war.

On weekends we'd go down into town, to the hospital. Each evening we'd go back to the boarding school. By train. We spoke less and less. Afterward, we'd slam a bunch of schnapps, because that made it easier to joke around with our friends.

That February, when Steffi came to take over for Mom in the hospital, Dad was doing really badly. Over the previous weeks, his strength had diminished to such a degree that I'd bawl in Mom's arms every time I left his room, and ask her why he wouldn't really talk to me anymore, why he was sleeping so much, even when I'd come to visit. The cancer was running wild inside him.

Steffi hadn't seen him for weeks. She'd been home alone, hitting the books. I was so thrilled she had finally come, I didn't even notice her terror when she finally saw Dad.

She and I stepped out of his room so we could catch up for a bit. Johannes sat at the bedside, one hand holding Dad's, the other holding his vocabulary book, although he didn't even glance at it once. Mom sat next to him. We sisters took the elevator down to the ground floor, walked past the cafeteria, and past the display cases with Nepalese jewelry. For the hundredth time, the automatic sliding-glass doors detected our motion and quietly slid open, and out we strode, into the cold winter air and across the parking lot to Mom's car.

The huge lot was virtually empty. A few bare trees with heavily pruned branches rose from the pavement here and there. The parking attendant's kiosk was shuttered, and the ugly seventies-era clock tower on the edge of the lot was mute.

We sat in the parked car. I can still remember how the air in Mom's VW Golf smelled as we got in – a little sour, like something fermenting (probably from the wine that had once spilled in the trunk), like damp upholstery, and like our dog, mixed with the sweet scent of strawberry and raspberry from the bag of gummy candies we'd bought at the gas station on the way. We sat in Mom's car in that vast parking lot in front of the huge white hospital complex, and I savored the few square feet of home that enveloped us. I told Steffi about school, boys, my girlfriends, and how Mom had defended me when one of the boarding school priests had insinuated that one had to be extra vigilant with me when it came to interactions with the opposite sex.

"What did she say to that?" Steffi asked.

"I don't know exactly, something like 'One must be extra vigilant with one's own projections,' or something along those lines. She was pretty upset."

I told Steffi that I'd talked to Dad about all of us going back to Spain again soon. "I'll take care of the flights. I promised him. That's what the So-and-sos – what's her name? – it's what my classmate Britta did with her family. She organized a trip to Russia. I'd like to do something like that too. I think Dad would be glad to get a bit of sun again. At least, he nodded when I told him I'd find the number of the travel agency."

Steffi didn't say anything back. She just gaped at me, wide-eyed.

"Esther," she said loudly, and then hesitated, as if she expected my name alone to convey what she meant.

"Dad's *dying!*" Her emphasis fell on the second word.

I still remember the moment vividly – that exact time in the car with Steffi, as opposed to so many others – because in the seconds that elapsed there, I realized how I was utterly unable to disagree. I didn't think Dad would die, but I also hadn't found a positive way to express that. I couldn't say, "God loves Dad, he has a plan for him, he just wants to test our belief, that's why he let him get sick. Dad will get better, because . . ." I had no positive way to express that. I stared at Steffi. She stared at me. Suddenly I was seized with rage. Furious over the fact that anyone would try to override the logic by which my world functioned, I summoned the most valid argument I could, articulating the laws of nature, what was right, how things worked, and blurted out, "No! That can't be! It's impossible. He can't die. Steffi! Just imagine Mom, if Dad were to die. He can't die!" Who wants to be capable of imagining death? Who wants to be able to picture the life of someone she loves being snuffed out? I'd really like to know. You might as well try eating your own brain with a fork and knife.

More silence. Steffi stared, mouth agape. I did too. As if we'd each brought the other to a halt and were waiting for one of our two statements to start outweighing the other, so we could begin speaking again. We were as stuck in place as two roosters in the ring, each undecided between fight and flight. They just stand there, pecking. We stared. Basically, both of us were right. You can't wrap your head around the death of someone you love. But it was also true that Dad was on his deathbed. My belief that Dad would get better didn't mean I was repressing knowledge to the contrary. It was just a manifestation of the impossibility of conceptualizing death. Whenever I tried picturing Dad dead, or even just a human life being extinguished, I felt like I was jamming my finger down the throat of love itself, like I was choking my own father, myself, everyone, everything. It was impossible. I wasn't built for that. At least, at the time, it was impossible.

This was one of the main reasons for my believing, that day in the car, that Dad would get better. An empirical miracle seemed much more realistic to me than death, much truer.

"Oh, Esther," Steffi broke the silent stare with a sigh, leaned forward, and pulled me into her arms. She'd understood. She was older than I was. I gazed past her brown hair, out the window, at the gray parking lot. I was happy for the hug, but unhappy to be enveloped in it, because it felt as if some unproven assertion wanted to settle everything, wanted my understanding, wanted to hear me say, "Yes, Dad is dying." All I could do to counter it was freeze. Or flip out, grab a sword, and hold it to the throat of anyone who would dare tell such a lie about my father. We are our lives. When life is gone, we are gone. And that's the most audacious, ugliest thing anyone can say about anyone else: He's dead. If that's so, then fuck human dignity, fuck saving the planet, fuck posterity – since they'll all kick the bucket too – fuck the world, if death is real. I wanted to threaten everyone who would make such an assertion, and I wanted to forbid the world to make any such claim, as if they knew anything about my father. How could they? What do we know about anyone? What can we know? How can anyone say, "Esther, you have to let him go"? Go where? Exactly where am I supposed to let him go? I won't let anyone I love disappear into a void, and I won't let anyone who belongs to me be taken away by death. My heart rose into my throat.

"Then what's up with God?" I exclaimed, angrily wrenching myself from her arms. "I mean, it can't be, Steffi. God exists. You yourself know that. It can't just be a bunch of bull."

She said nothing. She looked off to one side, gnawing her lip. Then she nodded silently to herself, turned to me, and said, "We need to pray again, Esther. It's been so long since we prayed. Have you been praying?"

I shook my head. "Nope, I haven't, really. I couldn't. Just sometimes. But I can't believe God will let Dad die."

"I can't either." She turned her collar up against the cold. I was looking for my cigarettes.

"Open the window, at least," she said as I found a pack in my coat pocket, beneath my crumpled-up gloves, fished one out, and lit it.

"I hate that you smoke."

"I don't care," I said, blowing a cloud of smoke from the right corner of my mouth as I rolled the window down. She covered her nose with her scarf.

"Can you start the engine, so we stay warm?" I asked.

"That won't do a thing." She stared straight through the windshield. "It'd be a waste of gas. Anyway, I want to get back up to Dad." We fell silent. My cigarette quietly hissed.

I broke the silence: "I told God the other day that he should say something to me – about Dad. I was supposed to be doing my homework, but I was too upset." I took another drag.

"And?" Steffi asked, sounding slightly strained. It's unfair to start telling someone something special when she's annoyed at you, but it's equally unfair to ruin the cigarette someone's trying to smoke after just having realized that her father really is on his deathbed.

"As I asked God to tell me something, anything, I got the feeling that he actually wanted to." I looked at her. "That he was just waiting for me to ask or something, y'know?"

"Yeah, I think I do," she said, taking the scarf from her face.

"Then I noticed this Bible, one I had to buy for class. It was under all my other books. The spine said 'Bible' on it, in bold – as if to say, 'Hey, over here!' So I opened it."

She turned to face me. "And?"

"It said – I underlined it – well, I don't remember exactly, but the first thing I read went something like, 'If you say to this mountain, be lifted up and thrown into the sea, it will happen, if only you believe strongly enough. If only you pray without doubting, whatever you ask will have already come to pass.'"

"Mm-hmm." She was almost smiling, but only almost. And a deep furrow had appeared on her brow – although it disappeared the moment she stopped thinking about death. "That's awesome."

I nodded, took one last drag, and flung the butt out the window. It landed on the pavement. I rolled the window back up. "I believe it," I said softly.

"Me too," she said, and we looked at one another. "Let's pray again, the day after tomorrow, when I get back to the cabin," she said, as her left hand felt for the door handle. She opened the door, and turned her back to me. She already had one foot on the ground.

"I'm so glad you're here," I said, and she turned around and hugged me.

"Me too," she murmured into my scarf, "but you stink of smoke."

From that day forward, I put all my trust in God. I gave him every ounce of faith, and began believing that the mountain would rise up and be cast into the sea – that Dad would get better – because I prayed as if it had already come to pass. Every last doubt dissipated. "Thank you, God, for wanting to help us. Thank you for bringing Dad back to health." I spoke to the God I had glimpsed on that beach in Spain. I gave him the belief I'd had in him since early childhood.

And six months later, my wailing echoed throughout the hospital and I felt I was going insane, that I had to tear the skin off my face, as my father lay dead in front of me. After that, a silence enveloped the whole world. It was quiet and cold. Like just after snow has fallen. No God. No me. No emotions.

WHITE AS SNOW

2

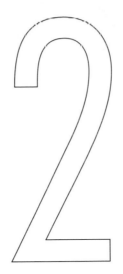

1

Insanity is when you have to kick all the doors in to get to the heart of the house, its core: the tiny, tough, everlasting atom, the only nucleus where you can save yourself. When the seconds open up behind you like a gaping hole, and the ground crumbles under your heels and falls into an abyss. You run through the house screaming, winding yourself up so you can kick the doors down, but someone has already carefully unhinged them. So your foot strikes nothing, the same nothing already tugging at the back of your heels. All your force meets with no resistance, and you stagger forward, plunging into the white void.

But insanity is not death. It isn't the end. It isn't some final breakdown. People are still around and able to hold on to a cup of coffee afterward, but it's no longer worth it. The passing seconds form a space that is long and hollow and round. It isn't death and it isn't the end. It's what happens when people crack, scream, and fall to pieces because they've seen their loved ones die, or because they find their kids lying dead in the street, or who knows what else has happened. It's not their death and it's not the end of them. They often still have many years ahead. They hear the clock tick. They hear a car drive by. Then they hear a song in the supermarket – a song they recognize from the old world, the time before – and wander on, bewildered, behind their shopping cart.

You still brush your teeth, but when you taste the toothpaste you wonder why. You might intuit that such a taste is just the nature of toothpaste, but you no longer understand why. Toothpaste doesn't belong to you anymore, it's foreign. You can tolerate the minty taste it leaves in your mouth, but you don't want it. Everything becomes so irrelevant that you are dumbfounded by the strange objects surrounding you – things that in the old world were everyday objects so familiar that you didn't even notice them. You're bewildered not just by things, but also by the things you do. You wash your hair. Your hands know, more or less, how to do it, and you let them do it. Sometimes you draw a blank and just stand there, confused, unsure what comes next, and forget why you're standing in front of the fridge holding a mixer, or why, all of a sudden, you're just sitting on the stairs.

The things of this world don't sound right anymore. There aren't any harmonies, nor any logical melodies to help you find your way.

It happens every day, in every corner of the world. Every day, over and over again, the world caves in on itself and we don't hear it.

God lets it happen. And many who've never believed in him consider this corroboration and say, "See? There's no one there. There never was. Death and suffering happen like the weather. When it's cold, people freeze, and when it gets colder, they freeze to death. We're unable to survive things. We're part and parcel of those things. Fire burns us, ice freezes us, and when our cells mutate we're devoured by them. If people have nothing to eat, they'll starve. No matter how hard their minds fight it, they'll starve to death. That's how the world works. That's how we work. Only our intelligence can save us. We can take precautions, protect ourselves, and develop systems that protect us from hunger and cold and disease and war. And we can shield ourselves from other people who go ballistic because they grew up in broken systems and families. But there never was anyone there, and there isn't now, even if we'd like there to be."

I couldn't think that. I felt exactly like that, but I couldn't think it. After what we'd been through, I should have had my head checked, and my siblings should have too. Often you have to question your own sanity, reevaluate things, rethink things, and so forth. But rethinking doesn't mean saying, "I told you so. It's that simple: your father is dead. There's obviously no God." I couldn't think that. It wasn't so simple.

All of a sudden, there I was, standing at Dad's grave like an idiot with a bouquet of flowers, and I no longer understood life, the world – anything.

Death didn't fit with what I'd understood up in the attic. It didn't fit with the sheer affection that all-encompassing power had shown us. I couldn't reconcile death with the astonishing realization that that power knows so much about each of us, and that each and every little crumb of experience, every fear, every secret and undefined feeling of ours had a place in it, and had long since reached that place. All these things couldn't have left this power, this God, untouched.

And, above all, one thing in particular didn't fit: the power I had experienced up in the attic, that calm love, was good. No matter how many philosophy books I was offered, no matter how many clever thoughts they contained claiming that God is everything and nothing and so on, it wouldn't have mattered. He was good. And that goodness had a certain authority simply because it was so good – I can't really explain it. Had it kneeled down on the ground next to a bird just to look at it, then everything behind it – every tree, every raised fist, every thought, all things – would bow down with it, as deep as God bows, down to the blinking sparrow. Things don't have to; this God doesn't command it. But they do, because he is good. Following him, everything comes to pass. He does not force it. Everything comes to pass in the same way that love comes to pass – it wants to and must be consummated. It bows down, gets up, follows, and isn't afraid of losing itself. It carries out every inhalation and every exhalation of everything and, in so doing, remains what it is.

God is good. Things follow him. Even if they don't want to, I realized, he can still force them to. They belong to him. They come from him. Even things that oppose him – he can force them, too.

This God – more real and so much tougher than an atomic nucleus, stricter and consequently more commanding than mutant DNA, freer than human law – he could, in all his kindness, have forced the cancer to retreat. He could have. Of that I was sure.

So why hadn't he? It made no sense in light of Dad's death.

2

My brother stayed at boarding school. My sister started college in Hamburg, and I moved back in with my mother, in the house we kids had grown up in. We took my grandmother in, too. She was ancient and had gone blind. Because she could no longer bathe, get dressed, or eat on her own, Mom and I cared for her.

Mom says that Grandma's presence after Dad's death was good for her because it helped fill the void in her life. She was needed. It was good for me too. Not the feeling of being needed, but of having a safe space – a place where I didn't have to be a teenager, where I didn't feel pressured to have fun and party all the time.

A person's inner landscape suffers when it clashes with the outer world. When you're lovesick, you can't enjoy being around couples who are always kissing. When your inner music falls silent, it's soothing to be somewhere that isn't too loud. That's why it was a relief to sit by my grandmother's bed, silent, staring, watching her breathe. The silence in that house suited me for a long time.

3

One night I woke up. It was one of many similar nights after Dad's funeral. I had dreamt of him. But then I had woken up, and in the sluggish fog between being awake and still asleep – as my consciousness swayed to and fro, from the realm of my dreams to the real darkness of the room – I suddenly heard a sound. Coming from the wall across from me. "That's what woke me up," I thought, and sat up to listen. It immediately stopped.

I groped for the switch on the bedside lamp, and as I felt along the cord, the scraping noise started again. When I paused to listen, it fell silent again. I turned on the light and leaned over on top of the pillows. The feathers rustled. Behind the wall, silence.

In my dream, Dad was sitting in the driver's seat of his car, his arms hanging down on either side of the steering wheel. He was dead. We kids were sitting in the back seat, I in the middle, Steffi on the right, Johannes on the left, and my mother in the front passenger seat. The car was driving itself through the hospital parking lot, which was now a cemetery full of gravestones. We hadn't chosen a tombstone yet. That's what we were doing in the dream. I said, "It's so awful we have to do this here. That he's dead, and that we have to engrave that fact in stone." We were all silent and sad. The car began turning, taking a curve, as if it were being steered along rails. Suddenly

Dad's lifeless hand, which otherwise lay motionless on the center console, twitched. It startled me. I leaned forward, stared at the hand, and thought: "Please, please, please, be alive. Please, move again." That's when Dad turned around, still a corpse, and said without speaking, "Esther, I'm always close to you. So close –" He extended his index finger, and it almost touched my arm. A cigarette lighter would have just fit into the gap. I looked at his finger and my arm. "But I cannot and must not come any closer." Then he turned away again, dead, and darkness enveloped me. That's when I woke up, opened my eyes, and came back to reality in my bedroom, and heard that soft scraping sound.

What can anyone make of such dreams? I didn't want them. I didn't like how they affected me. Virtually every bereavement book has something about these dreams.

No streetlamps shone outside. Our large stone house was quiet. My mother lay downstairs, in the double bed my parents had shared, breathing. In the next room over, Grandma lay breathing, her eyes closed. None of us really knew what we were doing, but that doesn't matter when you're sleeping. You don't have to know why you're here. You just sleep. You wait for time to heal your wounds. You breathe in and breathe out. You cleanse your soul by breathing.

I turned onto my side again, switched the light back off, and pressed my face into my pillow. Quietly, with my mouth right on the pillow, I whispered, "Dad." Such a natural, intimate word.

I waited. Silence. Just the echo of my shaking voice. I no longer really knew how to pronounce the word. Carefully, once again, "Dad."

Nothing but the room. The slope of the roof. The pillow. The pillow's scent.

"Dad," soundlessly swallowed up by the carpet or the duvet.

And as I lay there just wanting to slide away again – from one night right into the next, off to somewhere with real, deep sleep, where you didn't have to put up with your own consciousness – my wakefulness slowly clouded over, and I heard that scratching behind the wall. A bit farther away this time, and quieter. It irritated me, but I was too tired to kick the wall. It went on scratching and gnawing, utterly undisturbed. I fell asleep to it.

4

I didn't look up toward God. Scolded children only really look their parents in the eye if they already disdain them. I didn't disdain God – I was ashamed. For him and for myself. None of us kids talked about God after Dad's death. Our silent dealings with one another – the quiet glances we exchanged while we washed up, as we handed each other our plates – contained not only the shock and exhaustion of all the time he'd been ill, but also the indescribable self-delusion of our shared prayers.

But Tota talked about God. Tota was from Bosnia, and had helped my mother with household chores when we could still afford it. Of all of us, she might have been the only one who really had permission to speak about God. "Oh, little one, the dead are all still with us," she said to me, her face beaming, her dark eyes shining. She held my face in her hands, as she always had before I went off to boarding school. "My little one!" She kissed my cheeks and forehead. I couldn't look at her. "Esther" – her gaze sought mine. "We'll all be together when the time comes. Your lovely father – we'll all be so happy!" She cradled my face tight. I couldn't say a word.

Tota was a Christian. She was the only one in the house who really had permission to talk like that. She could say anything. She had been through hell in Bosnia, and when she talked about God it sounded more realistic than the horrors she'd seen. My father used to give her a Christmas bonus, and half an hour later you'd find her in town with her arms full of presents she was sending back to Bosnia. She'd laugh and say, "We're like little birds, we don't need anything – only freedom." I loved Tota.

And she was the only one who really had permission to talk about Dad like that. I never dared question it, but I also couldn't look at her as she spoke. I can't really say why. It was like everything faded away.

Every now and then a thought of God would pop up for a second, but it quickly vanished, and I was left alone again.

Mom had no idea how we were financially. She had become a homemaker when we were born. Dad had his company. If I had to paint a portrait of my mother in the year after Dad's death, it would show her buried under a mountain of files and paperwork. She'd be lying under it and ever so softly asking a question nobody could understand.

We should have gotten veils – black veils for widows, like in the olden days. That's how widows would stand by their loved ones' graves. But they don't anymore. It's seen as overly sad. Exaggerated, ridiculous. But these veils still exist. Whether you see them or not, they're still there. I don't know a single bereaved daughter who doesn't remember the delicate feel of them on her forehead – the darkened gaze. Whether you want to tear them off or not, they flutter against your face as long as your mother's wearing one.

In the fall and winter after Dad's death, Mom didn't turn the heat on at home. Out of fear that she'd need to start saving, she skimped everywhere she could. So it was freezing cold in every corner of the house, except in

Grandma's room, and the lights were only on in rooms where one of us was doing something.

At first, she sometimes accidentally cooked for five people. I remember looking at five portions of fish on a platter on the table and feeling a little embarrassed for her. She noticed, sat down with a sigh, folded her hands, and briefly closed her eyes, but didn't pray. Instead, she pulled Grandma's wheelchair closer to the table, tucked her napkin into her collar, and began to feed her.

When Grandma didn't eat, or when she started coughing after every sip of water, or when the fork near her mouth irritated her and she tried to shoo it away like a fly, Mom sometimes lost it. She'd slam the fork down on the plate and groan, "Esther, you take over. I can't do it anymore." Without a word, I'd begin deboning the fish and mashing the potato for Grandma. When I looked at Mom, I'd see that she was crying. I'd put the fork down again, walk around the wheelchair, sit down next to Mom, and hug her. Giving her a squeeze, I'd say, "Mom," and hold her briefly, only to realize that my embrace couldn't provide the consolation and protection she needed. It couldn't say, "Everything will be fine." Only Dad's arms could have. Mine offered no comfort, no protection.

Still, Mom's grief bound us together. She didn't cry often, but you can tell when someone's fighting and screaming internally, keeping it all pent up. We kids started giving her oversized gifts. We'd scrape together our pocket money to buy her opera tickets and red roses like Dad would have.

It became hard to get up, hard to watch a movie. I practically stopped hanging out with friends. I couldn't. We didn't have anything in common anymore. People would say, "You and your mother, you can't keep it all in; you have to let your pain out," and I could only think they had no idea what they were talking about. What pain? Dad had only been dead a couple of weeks. I didn't even miss him yet. At first there was only death. And it didn't hurt right away. It was just severe. It took away all the surfaces anything could stick to. Every line my spirit felt like writing no longer had a blackboard – the chalk just clicked, as if I were trying to write on glass, and left no trace. Nothing held. Every line I'd try to draw, every curve, whether whimsical or focused and precise, would slip away. I felt stupid.

Before that, I hadn't known the power that terror has, nor the power that death has – how strong they are against life. You have to raise your hand to your upper lip every now and then just to make sure it's there, because it feels like it has fallen asleep. German uses the same word for deafness and numbness, but numb is the perfect description for this feeling, this lack of feeling. It sounds so helpless, like you're groping for language that's adequate. It sounds like a toddler's mumbling, which is fitting when you're trying to describe people who've gone through such a terrible scare. People who are no longer functional. No longer participants, they become uncomfortable observers of the world. They look at the wrong things, are easily distracted, and their eyes get stuck on trivialities, like little kids marveling at cars driving by. It's uncomfortable for everyone around them. That's why Mom and I stayed home, both of us on our own. And when we went to bed, or said goodnight, we hadn't really experienced or lived the day. We had just gotten through it. Now it was over. But it would begin all over again tomorrow, and the next day.

5

I woke up again in the middle of the night, and yet again I had dreamt there were people standing in our yard, looking at us – another person every ten yards or so.

"Get out of here!" I had shouted. "Go away!" But they had just stood there, motionless, staring. Then they'd taken a small step forward, toward me, toward the house. "You need to go! Right now! Get out!" Another step forward.

Out of the corner of my eye, I saw that someone had almost reached the patio. A girl. She was talking nonstop, softly, while looking me in the eye. I didn't understand her, even though she was speaking my language. She took a step onto the patio and went on talking, slowly and quietly, still looking at me. I was yelling at her to go away. When she took another step, I ran into the house, grabbed the iron, swung, and knocked her head off. Her body fell over. I grabbed her head by the hair, yanked it into the air, and brandished it at the people in the yard. They all took another little step toward me. "You shouldn't be here," I yelled again. I was trembling with fear. I kept hearing their murmuring. Even though it was my mother tongue, it was utterly incomprehensible. It was coming from my hand or, rather, from the head I was holding by the hair. Its eyes had rolled back, but its mouth just kept talking. I wanted to cut its tongue out, but I couldn't get ahold of it because it kept wriggling. Then I woke up.

So I'm lying in the dark – it's the wee hours, though I don't know exactly what time it is. I have to get out of bed; otherwise, when I fall back to sleep, I'll fall right back into the dream, and it will continue. I know from experience.

Dad is dead, I suddenly remember. I'm sitting on the edge of the bed. The conversations about Dad having died, and still being dead, subside. As they fall silent, new conversations pop up – new questions to accompany the stupid old simple, smooth answers you give yourself as you bat around these questions each night. They all slump inward, trickling further into my head.

I get up, go downstairs, and immediately feel a chill. I'm drenched in the pungent, stinking sweat of fear; it permeates me like the dream. This god-awful trembling. The stairs creak as I descend. I don't turn on the light in the hallway, so as not to wake Grandma. I pause before her door and listen. I hear her breathing. I sneak down more steps toward the kitchen to get a drink, but then I hear something in the living room. The door is open. I cautiously peek inside and see my mother's silhouette in front of the window in the dark room. I stay on the threshold. She doesn't notice me, even though it's so quiet you can hear the softest breath. It sounds like she's crying. She's in her nightgown, standing next to the long, shadowy curtains, looking out into the yard. She loves Dad. That's why she's standing here in the middle of the night – because she loves him. Love always draws you in. When both people are alive, they're drawn into each other's arms. When one of them dies, the other one is drawn down the hall, into the outer rooms, and up to the window, where her breath fogs up the cold, glassy panes.

My mother's silhouette makes it seem as if my father is standing there, just outside the window. As if he were still here. Her round shoulders, her head, her petite body, the fall of her nightgown – everything leans toward someone, as if Dad were out there in front of the window, in the darkness of night, to reciprocate her love and comfort her. She holds her hand in front of her face, and her crying gets louder.

I walk away.

6

Pain can sneak up on you so quietly – smiling all the while, too. Even when you suddenly injure yourself (say you cut yourself), pain sits there patiently, just off stage, waiting in the darkness of the wings for eye contact, for a cue, until you grasp what has just happened. And then he steps forward slowly, steadily, self-confidently, arrogantly, ignorantly, even when he's booed. He makes his entrance with open arms: "Ladies and gentlemen, I'm pleased to…" Then he folds his hands, closes them knowingly, bats his eyes, and all the while he never loses his smile. Pain himself doesn't suffer. He's just there, running his own show. For hundreds of years now theologians and philosophers, or those who fancy themselves such, have been trying to interpret pain, understand him, and give him a role on the stage he has stepped onto without even auditioning. They're like a little *corps de ballet* dancing around their prima ballerina. Some of those in supporting roles even believe they're the directors. They tug at the star, saying, "No, that's not how it goes – with all due respect, allow me…" or try to shout past him, into the audience, "Pain is here because death was your father's redemption! Because your father suffered so much, it's better he died." And I shout back, "You call that redemption? Recovering would've been real redemption. What am I supposed to make of your little show?"

Then the dancers call back, "This drama will help you grow up! Just listen to what our clown has to say. Without him, we wouldn't know what a delight it is to enjoy a rational theatrical work. Without him, we wouldn't know what happiness is; we wouldn't appreciate it." And he's thrilled, patting them on their tutu-clad behinds. They don't even hear him say "Thank you!"

The audience gets angry, standing up to argue with the dancers, and everyone agrees the theater manager has gone mad. It's impossible – who let this clown in?

Some – no, almost all – of the philosophizing dancers concur that there must not be any manager whatsoever, given what a disaster this show is.

"The theater built itself!" someone shouts, while covering his ears because the clown is making deafening clicking noises as he nods. "This one," the dancer points to the clown, "is a part of the theater. He grew out of it; it's completely normal. He's just another piece of the building."

For a few seconds it's quiet. The clown morphs into a chair upholstered in red velvet and stands motionless in the middle of the stage. Some audience members in the back rows let out a relieved "Aha," and sit back down. The intermission vendor comes by, handing out little bottles of schnapps. The spotlights are on the ballerinas. The chair stands still, off in the dark. They tiptoe over to him, *en pointe*. The first dancer lifts him up, holds him overhead, does a pirouette, then passes him to the next one, and so on, and everyone dutifully nods. The children in the front row, though they were crying just a minute ago, are now applauding enthusiastically. Maybe their mothers are encouraging them to clap. Everyone is relieved: he's just a chair. But then there's a horrific bang because the chair has burst. He shouldn't be able to burst, should he? Well, he can, because he has cheeks he can puff up – and not just because he can, but because he wants to: because he might enjoy bursting, letting colorful confetti swirl through the air, before rematerializing again.

The ballet dancers are shocked that this self-built theater, with its clown-turned-chair, is behaving so unpredictably. Oh, what am I saying? Behaving? It's not like it has a will of its own. The dancers hold their hands in front of their mouths for a moment, open their eyes wide, and then blink their eyelids up and down, up and down.

But instead of retreating as far as possible, running off to cower in a corner, biting their nails and doing drugs until it stops, they start jumping higher and higher, pointing at the clown. They don't clap, no – they hate him – but now they're trying to convince the audience, by singing and gesticulating with their arms, shouting, "There's no manager at all – because of him!" For some reason this detail is important to them. Maybe it gives them meaning, who knows? Then they form a small circle around him, pointing to him. The kids start crying again, and their mothers hold them, praying, and whispering into their ears, "It's just a chair. Don't be scared; it's just a chair. You don't need to cry." But the kids, howling, reply, "He's a meanie."

A priest dangles in the chandelier – it's unclear whether he's Protestant or Catholic. He's got a white collar, but he tears it off his neck and waves it around in the air, saying, "What kind of manager do you have here, dear congregation? What kind of manager would allow something like this?" His voice trembles and he jabs his fists dramatically at the sky, then slips from the chandelier, though luckily his congregation catches, cradles, and caresses him.

The clown loves it. He puffs his cheeks out, squints, and holds his fists to his sides, tensing his muscles, and the word *rock* flashes across his forehead in green neon lights. And you can hear the audience marvel, some softly reading it aloud. "Hey, Werner, you see what it says there? What's that? *R-o-c-k*?" It piques their interest. "Oh yes, of course, mm-hmm," and they give a little nod, as if they've understood.

"Where's the manager, anyway? Why doesn't he intervene?" the priest whispers to his congregation, softly shaking his head. One of the more pious congregants says, "Maybe he's sick?" "Yes!" yells the priest, climbing back up to the chandelier and reclining as if it were a gondola. "That's it, ladies and gentlemen!" (Now he's addressing the whole audience, even though they couldn't care less what the guy up in the gondola has to say about anything.) "That's it! The manager is sick! There's nothing he can do about anything. He's down here among us, inside each of us. In our brother, our neighbor. He's a victim, just like us. He's made himself so small. He's just a sufferer, a victim like us!" Many in the audience nod sadly and pass it on, while others want to pull the priest down from the chandelier.

I consider getting involved, but then some ballet dancers rush over to help.

"I can imagine that there just might be someone up in the manager's booth. At least, you can't rule it out in principle," says a very delicate ballerina, her cheeks flushed with excitement because she believes she's found a solution. "But we can't say anything about what the manager is like. People can't know; that would be presumptuous," she says, shrugging her shoulders and curtsying, to great applause.

"What nonsense," snorts the man next to her, who has a fish on his sweater. "It says right here," he says, pointing at his program. Then he rolls it up and smacks her on the head with it. "Ouch," she says, and dies. "That's what you get," the man says, tapping his finger at his program again.

"Ladies and gentlemen!" yells the clown, pursing his lips and throwing kisses with his hands. And the newspaper will read, "This actor, Pain, this suffering . . ." And people will sit at their breakfast tables, shaking their heads and saying, "Why isn't anyone doing anything there? Pass me the coffee please, sweetie – starting tomorrow, we'll only buy fair-trade coffee." They'll say, "Why doesn't somebody do something? What's the manager up to?" Even if they've never been to the theater themselves, everyone gets very, very angry when it comes to the theater's manager, and everybody's talking. They all have a lot to say, and they go on talk shows, and they continue, "If there's really anyone up there in the manager's booth, how can he allow this?" In the end, many people decide there must not be anyone acting as manager after all, because it would all be too outrageously stupid if there were. And the people stuck inside – the ones who can't get out of the theater and who have to endure all this – the ones who've gotten to know the clown personally – nobody can ask them anything, because the show has already driven them completely nuts. Like me.

7

I had a seat in this shitty theater. On this particular day, it was a church. I was at a wedding. A few months had passed since Dad's funeral. The bridegroom was already on the steps leading to the altar. He smiled, then beamed, a little nervous. The old church – long nave, slightly clunky architecture, whitewashed walls – was full. The choir was at the back; the groom's parents were part of it. The sun was out because it was spring. Bright, white rays shone on the black, wet tree branches. I was later told that that same sunlight had appeared at Dad's funeral, as I stood next to the open grave, surrounded by all the businessmen in dark coats, who were trembling as they cried. Their sobs were softened by their sleeves, and I found it strangely exhilarating when they suddenly bent down like oversized children to hug me and hold me tight, even if they had never hugged me before. One buried his face in his wife's shoulder. She held him and carefully led him away. "My God," he whispered, "that child. God! Those children!" He raised his hand to his mouth. I watched him go. I had the feeling they all knew a lot more than I did, or understood a lot more. I had also noticed that people increasingly averted their gazes downward, or didn't dare to look straight at me. As if *I* had hurt them. I had become a little seventeen-year-old *memento mori.*

And now, in church for this wedding, I felt a little like that again. Many of the same suits that had sat in the pews at Dad's funeral were here too. Everyone knew my parents. They smiled at me sweetly, a little uncertain and inquisitive. They'd stop and say something to my mother, who was seated next to me. When I could react at all, it was only in slow motion. It takes so long to recover from such a powerful punch to the gut. My mother was friendly and looked right at people. I couldn't.

On top of the pain – a sensation that brings you back to life after a death, but only to make you suffer more – another feeling surfaced shortly before the wedding: anger. It was very timid at first, its pulse weak. Then it showed itself as pressed lips when someone tried to find meaning in Dad's death, or smilingly remarked on the flowers and mountains of wreaths covering the bare earth over the fresh grave, or saw the suffering of all his friends and relatives as a sign of their love.

I saw our suffering simply as suffering. I knew that I loved Dad before, and he knew it too. There was no point to his death. I couldn't explain why God had let Dad die – not after how we kids had prayed up in the attic with such deep faith. Sometimes I wondered whether my belief in God wasn't big enough. But then I thought, not even Peter really believed. He would have drowned if Jesus hadn't pulled him out of the water. So what kind of game was God playing with my faith, my trust?

You might think it's enough to just watch disasters unfolding on television, for example, to be able to honestly ask, "Why all this suffering?" But I'm not so sure about that. I think there's a difference between seeing something horrifying on TV that makes you intellectually wonder how God – if he exists – can let such a thing happen, and being incapable of even asking such a question because you've been so badly bruised that you yourself become a question. What if someone is so broken that she just caves in, slumping, her spine so broken and bent out of shape that it forms a question mark?

That's why I'd never be able to theologize or philosophize about the suffering I've seen on TV, nor could I offer anyone any general answers about suffering. I can't sit down in front of Catholics, Protestants, atheists, or any other of my fellow Germans who, in every conversation, seem so keen to try to solve the formula for suffering in their heads, either as offended interrogators or as arrogant responders. I can't compose any general formula for the clown, and anyone who says he can is a cynic. Nothing – not one of the various formulas I've heard – gets it right, and even if one could – well, it certainly wouldn't have come from anyone in the audience, in the *corps de ballet,* or at the breakfast table. Only the manager could have offered such a thing. But in all honesty, I didn't give a shit about the answer. I would've found any answer impudent. What could justify the desecrated corpse of a child? What good reason could ever explain Dad's horrific death?

No manager intervened, and God couldn't apologize either. There were no excuses because, if I knew anything at all about this God, it was that he had power and knowledge that encompassed the whole world, and someone who's all-powerful can't apologize for being weak or anything else. Regardless of what others might say, especially the priests who've been trying so hard to find excuses for him: "He can't right now, he's hanging on the cross, but his arms are open wide for us . . ."

So there I was, sitting in church, and staring straight ahead, past the bridegroom. I thought of my siblings and how we'd prayed – begged – God to let us keep Dad. I thought of Steffi's and Johannes's fingertips propping up their bowed foreheads, eyes closed, trying to hold themselves together and remain as calm as possible as they prayed, "Please, dear God, please don't let him die."

I thought of how, when Dad was losing ground, my voice had climbed higher as I'd said this sentence. I'd whimpered hoarsely, "Please! No, please, please, please, please, please, dear God! Let him live! I want to keep him, God! I'll do whatever you want, just please make him healthy again and let me keep him." My voice sounded just shy of throwing itself on the ground, like a whimpering mutt rolling on its back, tail between its legs. I thought of all my pale, used up prayers, and the foul smell of having cried for so long that your stomach is empty.

I thought of the moment when I'd prayed, "I believe in you, Jesus. Thank you for bringing Dad back to health."

I had done it, I thought, looking dead ahead at the altar, past the cross – I'd done *everything* any seventeen-year-old could do to trust and believe in God! I had tried so hard. I had tried like the people in the Bible. I had tried not to be an evil doubter. I would have removed the roof above him and let down a pallet with Dad lying on it. I would have stepped onto water; I would not have turned around. I would have crawled through a crowd on my stomach just to touch his robe. I would have followed a star. I would have listened to any stupid angel. I would have done all that, or at least I would've been ready to. I had prayed as if I had already received what I was asking for, and I really believed that God could heal him. And what did *he* do in return?

He'd said no. And not just no, but, "Nah, I don't know, I don't really feel like it right now." Actually, he hadn't said anything. Not one word. There might as well have been a huge black wall, so I could bang my head against it, though I guess I would have discovered that not even the plaster would crack, it was so impervious.

Suddenly the church organ cut through all these thoughts like a slap in the face. Everyone's heads turned – mine too – and there stood the bride in the arched doorway, resplendent in the spring sun, on her father's arm. He beamed with pride, and his every step emanated love and joy. His face shone with whatever it is fathers feel as they lead their daughters to the altar. I have no idea. They took two steps. She smiled, gazing happily toward the crowd. Her father looked at her from her side. Another step, and I saw his eyes shine, and the clown offered me his arm. And that's why I did the only thing I could. Instead of accepting yet another cup of tea and further debating the possibility or impossibility of the manager's actual existence, instead of philosophizing about the root cause of suffering or reproaching every second-rate believer – "Oh yeah? Well then, where was God when my father died?" – I got up, grabbed the clown by the hair, shoved him to the floor, and dragged him to the back of the stage, behind the curtain.

The bride walked past us with her father, and my mother put her hand on mine, but quickly pulled it back again. I don't know if she sensed my hatred as I stared forward. The clown giggled and cackled as I pulled him along. He made fun of me, covering my hands with kisses, slipping an engagement ring on and then yanking it off again, thanking my hands for their tenderness, grunting as he bowed his head beneath them, saying, "It's been a delight," and, "Thank you very much – I'm forever yours." I stood in front of the curtain and roared, just as the bride was given away by her father. And then I said to God, straight into the dark, that I hated him. I insulted him like you insult someone you want to hurt – someone you want to wound terribly – someone you want to goad into fighting back. And if that doesn't work, well then, someone you want to kill. It wasn't the sort of impassive hatred that teenagers feel toward their parents. This hatred encompassed my whole existence, my whole life, my whole world. And God.

I swore to him that I would never speak to him again, that I would hate him for the rest of my life.

The worst part was that I knew God was there. That certainty was very clearly there. My intellect required as much. "Tell me," I demanded, "What kind of pig are you, to not even *want* my belief in your miracles?" And then: "I don't believe in you anymore. You're dead. I hate you."

And then there was silence again.

8

The deer kept coming closer to the house.

One day after school I walked through the garden on my way to the patio and was surprised to see wooden poles sticking up out of the flower beds. They had small sacks tied to the top. Coming closer, I saw they were old nylon tights stuffed with hair.

"To keep the deer away," said Mom. "I got the clippings from the hairdresser. Supposedly they make it smell like someone's here."

It didn't help. The animals kept coming back and devouring everything.

Mom didn't talk about God. Although she suffered, and Dad's death had pained her, she was nevertheless buoyed by a solid faith. She told us kids once, before Dad's funeral, that as she was sitting by his bed the morning he passed away she had prayed, "Lord, if it is your will – if you really want him with you – then let it happen now, so he doesn't have to suffer any longer." Dad took a deep breath in; Mom said, "Amen." Then Dad breathed out and was dead. She didn't say anything about God, but that moment carried her, even though she could never tell us what it had really been like. The presence of God – that was it – and consummate love, all in a single room built of nothing but peace. She regretted we hadn't been there.

“It would have been such a comfort to you, Esther. I can’t adequately convey it. It was lovely.” But I didn’t want to hear about it. I just kept asking her what exactly he died of, over and over again, because I didn’t understand.

One day the pastor paid us a visit. We drank coffee out on the patio among the half-eaten roses. That didn’t help either. Every day that summer, my grandmother sat out there in her wheelchair with a big black sun hat over her white updo and huge, brown sunglasses. She’d chuckle whenever a blackbird got riled up and strutted indignantly through the garden, or purr “how beautiful” whenever one poured its heart out in a cascade of sweet chirps. She received communion from the parish assistant out on the patio under the red awning. Her blind eyes were closed. I sat across from her. (I stayed with Grandma all the time, so I was usually there when someone came by – visiting nurse, pastor, doctor – and I’d watch what they did with her.) I leaned back in my chair and watched, peering over my coffee cup, as Grandma opened her mouth and the parish assistant carefully placed a little white host on her tongue. She might have been confused about other things, but to my amazement she always looked as if she understood this. I drank my coffee, watching closely. I didn’t know what the little wafer was. And I didn’t understand the vast system that had sprouted up from this belief in God and Christ – a thousand intricate details governing belief. I was amazed at how much had been built up around it, and wondered why the whole shebang didn’t just blow up – why it didn’t fall apart, and how and why they could just carry on, paying parish assistants, sewing altar boys’ robes, baking wafers, pouring chalices of wine, printing flyers. God was evidently holding up so well that they could keep building the palace around him bigger and bigger. I didn't get it.

I wondered what God they knew about that I didn't, because mine was so massive and brazen, so there and not there, like this shitty blue sky, like this farcical fine weather and birdsong and buzzing little red beetles, drunk bumblebees, and daisies – and it was all as tasteful as the little buttonhole posy gracing Dad's ice-cold tuxedo in the coffin.

9

It was already dark by the time I left school. The air hung cold and wet over the poorly lit street. Our house was up on the hillside, where the road curved. A faint light was on upstairs, in Grandma's room. I rang, but Mom didn't open. The doorbell was no longer reliable; it didn't always ring. So I started rummaging through my bag for the key, which had slipped down between the pages of a book.

"Evening," I heard someone say behind me. A neighbor taking his dog for a walk.

"Hi," I said back. I unlocked the door, walked down the dark hall, and looked into the living room. "Mom?" No answer. I turned on the hallway light and climbed the stairs. "Mom?" There she was, sitting on the floor outside her bedroom door, her face in her hands. "Mom?" I sat down next to her, "Something happen?"

"Oh," she said, waving it off with her hand and then rubbing her face. Then she stood up and said, "Nothing – it just reeks in there." She fumbled for a handkerchief, and blew her nose.

"What is it?" I asked. I was now sitting down there on the floor by myself for no reason.

"Nothing," Mom repeated. And then, stubborn as a child: "I'm *not* going back in there again. Someone else can get rid of it. But not me. I can't do it anymore." I got up to hug her.

"What's going on?"

"Something died behind the closet, some animal or something," she said with a dismissive gesture. She freed herself from my hug and went down the hall. You could hear Grandma's soft voice, and then my mother's, which now sounded more controlled. I tossed my bag down and opened the door to my parents' bedroom. It was dark. You could see the outlines of their bed, covered in a light-colored bedspread – one part flat on the mattress, the other part with a bulge made by Mom's blanket and pillow. The balcony door was open. Gusts of cold air blew through the darkened room, but even the wind couldn't sweep that sickly sweet, faintly rotten smell away. I went into the bathroom, washed my hands and face with soap, and brushed my teeth. I understood why Mom had reacted as she did. She slept in Johannes's room that night.

The next day I removed several drawers from Mom's and Dad's built-in closet. The stench got stronger, and I wrapped my scarf around my mouth and nose, pulling it so tight that my nose was pressed flat in front. I couldn't find a flashlight, so I plugged a bedside lamp into an extension cord and held it in the space between the closet and the outer wall.

The glare of the lamp immediately revealed a mouse nest between the beams and the masonry. There were seven mice in it. All dead. It looked like they had been eating the insulation in the wall behind the closet – the nest was surrounded by little chewed bits of yellow fiberglass. Paper towel in hand, I lifted the small, hard, cold bodies out. As I went downstairs to toss them into the woods behind the garden, I thought: Someday I'll stink like that, too, and be stiff and cold, and something will be oozing out of me. Where will I be then? Where does everyone go? There's got to be some little shitty reason for having hope, right? Even without God. If not, why don't we all freeze our bodies when we die. Maybe science will revive us one day.

I got to the fence, twisted up the paper towel the mice were in, and threw the bundle as far as I could into the woods. Somewhere back there, they landed with a plop. I strode back over the cold grass to the house and past our old kiddy pool, whose edge was cracked from when the retaining wall above it had collapsed the previous year, back when Dad was in the hospital. Everything here was broken, including the whole logic about dying, and whatever comes after it, or doesn't. How did other people handle it? How did they do it? How could they stand anything if there were no heaven? Why wouldn't they make provisions, prepare somehow? What answers did they have?

I crossed the wet, cold, dark lawn, and the patio emptied of all furniture, and went through the patio door. It was all so stupid. Life – all intellect and culture and death – was really enough to make you want to eat your own brain. As I went to open the door, our dog started barking like mad, baring its aged teeth.

I walked in, but he didn't stop barking. "You okay?" I asked. He stood in front of me and growled, then slowly circled me and barked twice more. I snarled at him. His face relaxed and he wagged his tail happily.

Five minutes later, my grandmother bit the public health nurse.

Mom had just come into the kitchen and was standing at the sink, when suddenly this young woman, who was always so nice to Grandma, called down from the landing, "Hello?" My mother dried her hands and stepped into the hall. "Yes?" she said, looking up the stairs. The nurse was leaning against the top railing and holding her finger. "Your mother . . .she . . .well, she just bit my finger."

The nurse's voice shook. She was about to cry. Mom, appalled, called out, "She did what?" I left the kitchen and joined them. "What happened?"

"She bit Veronica," Mom said to me.

"Who did?"

"Your grandmother." I nearly collapsed with laughter. The nurse had already disappeared back into Grandma's room. Mom shot me a stern look and said, "Come, Esther, stop now, that's inappropriate. She can't just bite her nurse." I howled with laughter. "I know," I said. "Anyone else, go ahead – but please, not Veronica!" I was almost squealing, it was so hilarious. I laughed so hard I cried. I stayed at the bottom of the stairs, and had to sit down. Mom shook her head and headed upstairs, serious – furious. And then I heard her scolding Grandma.

"Mother dear, that's no good. You can't just bite Veronica."

I ran upstairs, briefly paused outside Grandma's door, and tried to collect myself so as not to immediately lose it again. Inside, Grandma sat gracefully in her pink nightgown on her little chair, her teeth clenched.

"I told her I'd like to brush her teeth, and asked her to please give them to me, and she just bit me," said the nurse, her lower lip quivering. She was obviously deeply hurt. I felt bad for her, but that didn't make it any less hilarious.

"She probably just didn't want to give up her teeth," I volunteered, stepping into the room. "Or maybe she thought your finger was something to eat?"

But Veronica didn't believe any of it. Mom apologized to her and scolded Grandma again. The nurse called it a day. When the door downstairs clicked shut behind her, Mom began laughing and couldn't stop. She laughed and laughed, holding her stomach with her hand, and nearly doubling over. I did too. All this craziness was somehow good. Everything's gone nuts, I thought. The world doesn't stick to the rules of the game, and neither does cancer – nor Grandma.

10

At home, I mostly sat up in the attic, alone. Sometimes I'd stuff one of Dad's pipes with his old, dried-up tobacco, try to smoke it, and think of death. I didn't have any thoughts of my own about it. I'd never needed to, at least not before. My grandfather died when I was eight. After the funeral we had taken a walk in the woods. The ground was covered in red autumn leaves and there were mushrooms everywhere. I remember wondering where Grandad was now. I wondered whether this same path through the woods also existed in heaven, because – if the grown-ups were right when they said that he was still with us – then this path had to exist in heaven, or heaven was here. Or something like that.

That was basically the only conscious thought I'd had about death up until it took Dad. Of course, I'd also gone through a phase in the eighth grade or thereabouts where I found reincarnation more appealing than heaven and hell. I didn't believe in hell anyway. As a Catholic, you didn't have to. Nobody else really believed in it, either, except in the case of Hitler.

Reincarnation seemed reasonable. But the thoughts I had about it weren't exactly deep or far-reaching. My friends and I just figured that reincarnation sounded better, friendlier. And nobody had told us you could be reborn as a pebble. In any case, my notion of death was pretty undeveloped when Dad died.

"He lives on," Christian friends and family members said. I knew that already. With God, not a soul gets lost. And I thought, "Yeah. We live on. That's how I'd like things to go, too. And while you're at it, I'll take a house made of cotton candy, and please only let people I like into heaven; so, just four or five max. Thanks."

I wanted God to just disappear from my mind. I wanted to tidy up all the loose ends and live in a mentally clean house. That would include, first and foremost, admitting that life ends with death. But that was awful. In fact, it struck me as a terrifying idea, and I ventured toward it as if on thin ice. I wasn't so sure at the beginning either. As I said, I hardly had any original wisdom on the matter, so I gleaned what I could from the outside world and then elaborated on it. I listened more closely when the topic of death came up in conversation. When my mother went channel surfing in the evenings and ended up on a talk show, I would immediately perk up whenever existential questions were broached.

Staring at the TV one night, I saw someone smiling and saying that nothing comes after death. It wasn't the statement, but the smile that really got to me. It made me suspicious. I saw it a lot, and not just on TV. I'd often heard it said, or hinted at between the lines when adults were talking. I couldn't take it. It threw me for a loop that such pronouncements were considered a worldview, accompanied by an intellectual gesture, rather than ideas triggering total despair. I didn't know if I was the one missing something, since I just couldn't accept this "fact" yet, or if they were the ones missing something. Where was their sadness? Why did they seem so confident? They had no reason to be. They were self-proclaimed maggot fodder. I might have been ready to see myself that way too – but then life had to be livable. That's what I was looking for at the time. These people cannot believe what they are saying, I thought. And if they do, then they must have some superhuman power, or they don't love anyone, not even themselves. But they smiled too much for that.

Even before Dad's death, I was suspicious of adults who, in my eyes, seemed to live in a way that didn't match what they claimed to believe. Somehow it always grated on me.

Back in the eighties and nineties, in my childhood and teenage years, it was trendy to be unable to believe in God, and to point out with a sigh that you couldn't just ignore science. I remember feeling stupid when the topic came up at dinners, and sometimes I'd squint at my parents and wonder if all the hobby biologists at the table were actually in silent agreement that my churchgoing parents were a little dumber than they were. One time it escalated. I was fifteen and attending one of my father's business dinners with my parents when the anger erupted in me for the first time. After Dad's death it grew even stronger, especially toward the older generation.

There were about ten of us, and we were seated at a round table. I don't know why my siblings weren't there. A heavily starched white napkin loomed on the plate before me. Next to it stood two wine glasses and a water glass. They sparkled with the reflection of the lights overhead.

The women smelled of perfume that evening, the men of after-shave, and later on their smiles revealed bluish teeth from all the red wine and cigar smoke. Since they all knew each other well professionally, and the business part of the meal was merely intended to confirm that everyone was still on the same page, the conversation soon meandered, as usual, from economics to politics to society and art and then to religion – which wasn't the most fitting topic for the situation. But so it went.

I clearly remember one of the men – very tall and a bit stocky, slightly graying, around sixty years old – leaning back in his chair, puffing on his cigar as the rest of the table talked about God.

I no longer remember what triggered his monologue, but I remember his main point. He was talking about theories: the Big Bang, evolution, that humans are highly developed animals, and so on. It wasn't the commonplace verbiage you so often hear. This guy sounded good.

People generally seem to enjoy tossing the term "Big Bang" into any conversation about God, and if you play dumb and straightforwardly ask, "What kind of big bang?" the answer is usually, "Well, you know – the Big Bang." And then you're apparently supposed to reply with something like, "Oh right, of course," even though you now know the other person is just as unclear on it as you are. Then you just have to endure the next few minutes as they recklessly juggle elephants. If you're not up for that, and stubbornly ask again, you get answers that would've gotten a big fat F in ninth-grade physics.

But it wasn't like that here. This man spoke at length. He delved deep into his worldview. He sounded confident. Everyone listened attentively. His wife sat next to him, visibly proud, and he spread out in his chair as he spoke. Then he brought up the indemonstrable nature of God and how, since no one could prove his existence, it is stupid that people believe in the human soul, not to mention immortality, not to mention God. Science would soon explain all of it. He said it with confidence and conviction – like a man of the world.

I hadn't been a passionate believer before Dad's illness, but I had also never seen human existence as a biological accident; I had never denied the existence of God or of a creative higher power behind nature. To do so struck me then as unreasonable. It seemed to me to be a somewhat medieval way of thinking, one in which people imagine that they are the center of the universe and then go about constructing elaborate hypotheses based on what they take to be scientific fact. This thought occurred to me for the first time when I saw an exhibition with my parents. It was about Max Planck. There was a photo of him and a bunch of other illustrious men, all gazing at the camera from bearded faces with excited eyes, confident and proud. And then I read somewhere that someone had told Planck to give up studying physics because all the great discoveries had already been made, and there were no new ones left, as if to say, "The earth is flat. That's it."

Anyway, a certain suspicion came over me as I listened to this man at that business dinner. I remember feeling ashamed for him because he sounded so stupid, especially when I considered that most of what we humans consider knowledge is ultimately a belief in some set of preliminary findings. It annoyed me that he pretended everything was so clear. Actually, it made me mad, because his patronizing, self-satisfied chatter about the lowliness and insignificance of human beings, who to him were just some biological accident, belittled not just humanity at large but also the person sitting next to him: his wife. She was tipsy, smiling proudly, and clearly not fully catching on to what was being said. My heartbeat rose; I could feel it at the back of my tongue. I was getting worked up.

I swallowed hard. "Do you actually love your wife?" I heard myself asking him. The clinking of cutlery stopped immediately. The speaker glanced at his wife, who looked around the table and gave an uncertain chuckle. Then everyone chuckled, and I continued, "I don't believe you do. In any case, you can't prove it. All you can say is that her scent attracts you, and that your allegiance is the result of mere social pressure or self-interest, because you need warmth and security at home, and she's raising your offspring. If I were your wife, I'd be very sad."

I was lucky everyone had already had a lot to drink, and that my words were interpreted as angst-ridden adolescent cheek. People often confuse intelligence with rebelliousness. My parents didn't. After the meal I got an earful.

"You just can't say things like that, Esther," said my mother.

"But he insulted his wife. He insulted all of us at the table. If he thinks he's a monkey, then he should chow down his food straight out of a bowl, instead of holding a fork and putting on such airs as to stick out his little finger."

"That's enough," said Mom. "Next time you're staying home."

"Gladly. Thanks."

That was later, at home. Back at the table, all the other adults just laughed it off, except for Mom, who glared at me, and Dad, who raised his eyebrows. That's why I knew there'd be more to come.

"Ah, indeed – love! Now *there's* a topic," Mr. Soulless went on enthusiastically. Then everyone began drinking more wine and quoting great men of letters on how the heavens kissed the earth and the soul spread its wings and blah blah blah.

The helplessness and speechlessness underlying that generation's unbelief had always put me off. I couldn't stand their superficiality, their lack of logic, the contradiction between their supposed beliefs and their actual lives. And their self-conscious sighs and assertions – "I'm a critical thinker, after all" – didn't help. Ironically, these were the same people who cared about the media's take on everything – who followed whatever the paper's editor-in-chief had picked out over breakfast and turned into the topic of the day, and then accepted it as fact, as "knowledge."

For them, the Enlightenment was a historic event, which meant that as members of subsequent generations – children of the Enlightenment – they were automatically allowed to regard themselves as enlightened. They no longer had to shuffle around with a priest holding their hand. They were free to find support elsewhere.

I didn't want to be like that – neither before Dad's death nor after, neither with God nor without. And my aversion grew stronger. I didn't care to chime in on this pseudoscientific debate between my elders and my peers, who coyly referred to themselves as half-apes while straightening their ties, attending Beethoven concerts, and following the score. These people who viewed monogamy as a cultural imposition, and who saw sleeping with their wives only as the conventional way of ensuring the propagation of their genes, or of adding a dash of enjoyment – ahem, I mean endorphins – to their otherwise meaningless existence.

I didn't want to be like that. I figured it had to be possible to not believe in God, to understand death as the end of life, and to just deal with it in a dignified way. Others obviously could. Those who didn't believe life went on after death somehow found a way to accept it. Or so I thought. But then I saw the embarrassed fidgeting of unbelieving adults – an entire generation flailing about. I saw it more and more after Dad's death. At first it just unsettled me; then it began to disgust me, and I lost all respect for them. They were just pretending that they accepted death. In the end, they couldn't think of anything to do with it, except admit that it was somehow sad.

As my distress grew, I found the answers on offer increasingly cheap. I saw that death had a way of blowing people's fuses. Everyone – all these grown-up, adult, critical thinkers and realists – would earnestly quote *The Little Prince*, paraphrasing the comforting idea that whoever has died is now a star looking down at us. Yeah, sure. Thanks a lot.

"I believe your father is still with us, taking it all in," said people who I knew didn't believe in anything – but then suddenly did, or whatever.

"Your father is an angel now," said one woman, also not a believer. I wanted to ask her, "So is he a chubby little naked one, or is he one of the grown-up, nightgown-wearing, harp-playing ones?"

"We're still carrying him in our hearts," said atheists and priests – unbelievers and believers alike. It was meant to be consoling, but apparently they didn't realize how heavily another person can weigh on your heart, how impossible it is to bear that weight alone, and how idiotic it would be to take their words as the definitive answer to the question of where we go and what becomes of our existence.

It was all so degrading, so devoid of meaning. At least have the courage to say he's gone, I thought, and that in a hundred years no one, not a single person, will remember him; that it'll be as if he, you, and I never existed. That's what you really believe, isn't it? That's what you always say. Why all the lofty posturing?

The people around me didn't know where Dad was. And because they loved him less than Mom, Steffi, Johannes, and I did, they randomly shot him up into the sky as a star, or into the clouds as an angel, or tucked him away in the golden prison of their memory. Yes, a prison, because keeping someone in your memory is confining. It's like cramming him into a treasure chest brimful of your favorite toys and dolls. After two weeks, tops, you know all the games, the music boxes play all the same ditties, and you start going crazy.

Yet that's what society proposes we do with the dead. "He lives on in our memories." "In our hearts, he will never die." Bullshit! I couldn't listen to that anymore. What was all this talk about the heart, as if it were an exclusively honorable, sacred place? As if my father would be in good company there? As if we were all so incredibly loyal? As if the heart were a holy shrine in which a person could be truly captured and preserved? And all this coming from a society whose best attempts to describe the soul end in equating it with synapses, while the heart – the pumping lump of flesh under our ribs – is somehow suited to serve as a new heaven! Come again?

Anyone who loves someone is apt to be distressed when that someone dies. In a very real way, you want to know where that person has gone. Anyone who loves someone is distressed that death could turn that love into a bad joke, into something so aimless: the love remains, but its object is gone. So you are left with having to anchor this love somewhere in the past – you do things like have your dearly departed dog stuffed, or display your loved one's ashes in an urn on the mantelpiece, or make a shrine, or watch old videos of your deceased loved one, smiling and waving at the camera.

Whoever doesn't want to deal with death by taking that route has no choice but to let their love die along with the person who has died – in order for that love to be redemptive. Because if you no longer exist anywhere after you die, then my love for you is superfluous. It can keep neither of us alive. And so it just lingers, hanging there, weighing you down, making you stumble through life because it does not allow you to look forward. It constantly turns backward, longing and reminiscing, while simultaneously clinging to you, since it has missed its chance to go with the person who is gone.

If that's what love for the dead entails – that it should die with the beloved, even if very few care to admit this – well then, I didn't feel capable of saying anything about it.

Such love was foreign to me. The only love I knew demanded eternity. And if this love had been laid down in front of me, sooner or later I would have had to break its little neck. Because I wouldn't be able to stand its squalling. No one could. It would drive you crazy.

11

A bunch of teens dressed up in traditional African costumes jumped across the auditorium stage. Their movements lacked any of the elegance that the original dance they were trying to imitate may have had. These dancers were German, and they jumped and swung their hips awkwardly. Their whooping was also undeniably German.

Most of the time, I skipped chapel at school. The last time I'd attended, it was about female circumcision, and we were all totally shocked and concerned. This time it was just supposed to be happy. As the dancers shouted, "Jesus has a crush on you," and feedback from the microphones screeched from the speakers, I ditched the service, walked out to the courtyard, lit a cigarette, and hoped for their sake that Jesus wouldn't break up with them when the butterflies vanished from his stomach and the thrill was gone.

No sooner had I set foot in the empty yard than my restlessness returned, bringing with it the thought that it would actually be better to leave right now, and not to show my face in school at all. Then I could prolong yesterday's excuse, and it really would look like the flu. I had already missed one day, and then another, and then I'd come back for a day, gone to fourth period, and then gone absent again.

I knew perfectly well that it would end in disaster if I kept playing hooky, but I just couldn't show up. Going to school should have been a foregone conclusion, planted and rooted deep within my core, down where all the fundamental principles are, down where I'd been spending most of my time lately. But it was pretty bare down there. Not much going on. Almost everything had been swept away. There was a faint humming, and a few wounded butterflies flitting about, trying to land, but there was no ground for them to land on.

All the thoughts about life and death that were whirling around in me, all my grumbling about adult worldviews and about my surroundings – it was all just hoarse barking. I felt like some mutt guarding a barren playground where the swings and sand pits have been cleared away. Like I was watching over some empty space, and allowing nothing irrational in. I guess I thought I could think my way through the world. And only allow pure reality to enter my space.

I wanted facts. Since death is such a cold, hard fact, I decided, then life has to have equally cold, hard facts. I walked along the street bordering the school. There were a lot of trees and a few houses in between them. They had all been built after the war. I knew that there had been no town here before. There had been an armory. And then, after the war, a bunch of immigrants had arrived, and these houses had been built. First woods, then weapons, now homes, and in a few years we'll see. Things come and go. "It's all so ridiculous," I thought. "The bus always comes so dutifully and punctually. And when the bus driver dies, another driver who hates his job will come along, and my classmates and I will grow up, and then we'll die, and so on and so on and so on."

There wasn't a car in sight, but still I waited at the crosswalk, because the pedestrian light was red. Ridiculous. But going through a red light would have been just as ridiculous. Maybe walking is fundamentally ridiculous. So is breathing.

The bus came. It roared past me and stopped, the crossing light turned green, and I ran over, hoping the bus would wait for me. As I got to the door, it was already closing, but I squeezed through, showed my student ID, and sat down right behind the driver. I had to catch my breath.

Why so fast?

I tried to breathe slower. The bus was empty. The driver switched on the radio, bored.

I didn't want to wait another hour. I wanted to get home.

And then?

I don't know.

What's next?

Do good.

What does that mean? What's good? And for whom?

For me.

Who is that?

I just want to sleep.

What is the purpose of your life?

There is none. I have to make it up myself.

But that would not be real purpose then.

I just want to go to sleep.

12

"They've ransacked everything," Mom was saying into the receiver, clearly upset. She was sitting on the old Biedermeier sofa we had recently moved to the hallway, because Dad's old desk from the office had taken its place in the living room. I had just come home from school. I had been playing hooky again, though she didn't notice. When she saw me, she took the phone from her ear, tapped her arm, and pointed to the living room door. Following her signals, I opened the door and saw Grandma sitting in the armchair. A tube led from her arm to a plastic IV bag hanging from the chandelier, tied with a yellow ribbon. Whenever Grandma was on the IV someone had to hold her hand tight, because her veins were fragile and the needle could wreak havoc if she moved around too much. So that's what Mom's silent gestures meant: I was supposed to hold Grandma's hand.

The TV was on, but muted. I squatted down in front of Grandma, took her hand, and held it tight. "Hi there," I said.

"You have to pull the seams a little tighter."

I laughed. "I have to what?" I asked, and then she realized she was incoherent again.

"Oh, never mind. I was just babbling."

"It's okay," I said, and then we were both silent for a bit. Her other hand trembled as she groped at the arm that was hooked up to the IV – the one I was holding. I quickly reached for her roving hand with my free one, grasped it, and sat with my arms firmly crossed in front of her, not daring to let go, even as my school bag slid down off my shoulder and hung heavily on my forearm. I knew that if I let go of one of her hands for even a moment to put my bag down, she might hurt herself with a hasty motion. It was an awkward position, and my bag was heavy.

"You're such a sweetheart," she said suddenly, her blind eyes staring straight at my forehead.

"Mm-hm," I smiled. Just then my arm gave way, yanking downward. Her vein burst, the IV fluid began spreading under her skin, and her arm began swelling. "Damn it." I let my bag drop to the floor and clenched my hand around her thin arm.

Mom entered just then. She looked tired. A strand of hair had fallen from her barrette and was hanging in her face. She tucked it behind her ear. "They've destroyed my entire garden!" she said.

"Who?" I asked.

"Those stupid animals."

"What animals?"

"The pigs!" And then she saw me pull the needle out of Grandma's arm and dash to the chandelier to twist the little plastic knob to shut off the drip. "Oh, c'mon," she moaned, irritated. "You *have* to twist it shut up here first, before you take the needle out."

"Oops, I forgot."

The smell of disinfectant stung my nostrils as I sprayed the gauze with it and stuck the bandage on Grandma's arm with a piece of sterile tape. "So, you're still hanging around, huh?" I thought. "You awful, reeking, medicinal stench. You're going to keep haunting us even now that

Dad is dead?"

Mom swore as she turned the IV bag in front of the light. Not even a quarter of the IV fluid had gone through. "I'll call the doctor again. He can come right back. It's not like I've got anything else to do today."

"What were you saying about stupid animals just now?" I asked.

"Just look out there," she said, angrily nodding toward the garden while examining Grandma's arm. "Wild boars – a whole herd. Go see for yourself."

I got up and went to the patio door, opened it, and stepped outside. The sky was cloudy and gray, and it was dusky enough that at first I didn't even see what Mom was talking about. But when I took a few steps into the garden, I realized the entire upper portion, even our two flower beds, had been plowed up. The ground was all dug up. Going a little farther, I saw that the bottom of the garden, where the apple trees were, was the same. Everything had been uprooted, churned up; the surface was no longer level. It was ugly. Even the fixtures holding up the big net Mom and I had so laboriously stretched over the pond in the fall, so that leaves wouldn't fall in and make everything mucky, had been toppled by the wild boars.

Heavy with wet leaves, it had sunk into the black water.

We didn't clean it up. That winter we just let it all freeze, exactly as it was.

13

The snitch came by in secret. She was almost elegant, and so polite that she never looked directly at me. She just asked questions, and I answered them. I thought it was *me* that was thinking – that it was just *my* thoughts. Back then I still believed in such a thing: the possibility of pondering the existence (and potential absurdity) of humankind, life, and death in solitude. But the mind is actually never alone. You always have company when you're thinking, even if you don't realize it.

Somehow thoughts find their way into reality. At least so I had thought, after going to see Dürrenmatt's satire *The Physicists*, where one of the characters says, "Once you've thought something, you can no longer take it back." But it didn't occur to me at the time that there obviously had to be someone who could betray such thoughts.

The snitch came by in secret. I don't know when. She took no interest in me, but she stayed anyway. Almost loyally. Actually, I have to admit that it wasn't a conversation. I think she was counting. Maybe seconds. I don't know. She was death's little sister, or his babysitter. Or maybe he was her pimp. I don't know. Anyway, she was counting quietly the whole time, and whittling away at something. I had no idea she had such a nasty agenda – that in her quiet, pleasantly determined way, she managed to make people jump from skyscrapers, or gingerly nudged them onto train tracks. And I had no idea that it wasn't really possible to argue with her. That wouldn't have been her style; she lacked the necessary passion.

"If life ends with death," I reasoned, "then you just have to make the best of it."

She merely smiled.

"Just because there's no God doesn't mean our entire existence has to be absurd. And even if it is absurd, I can still make sense of it for myself . . ."

She almost grinned.

"I can make it have meaning for myself. If, in a few years, I'm no longer sad, then . . ."

She wasn't even listening.

"I have a name, a personality, a will of my own!" I barked at her.

She paused, smiled, and kept on whittling away at whatever it was, as if she hadn't heard a thing.

"I have a mother, a sister, a brother – they would miss me. I'm registered, you hear me? I have an ID, see? There are records proving my existence. I am a person. I have basic human rights; they're in writing. I belong here. I'm important. I've done some good for people, I've made the world a little bit better here and there. That's meaningful! That's a good thing."

She didn't even raise her head as I said it. She didn't look up until she'd finished whittling away at the hole through which my arguments were now trickling.

"That doesn't matter," she said smoothly, holding her hand out to catch the falling shavings. Then she smiled and repeated herself. "None of it matters now."

14

I went to the woods every day when I played hooky. Most of the time I'd go to the tower my siblings and I had dubbed Rapunzel Tower when we were kids, because it looked like something straight out of a picture book. Its base was circular, made of big, heavy, gray stones, complete with battlements on top and a spiral staircase inside. One of the battlements had broken off, and I'd sit on the stump for hours, smoking. You used to be able to see the city from the tower, but not anymore. The trees had grown too tall. Sometimes you could hear the train crossing the valley, its horn tooting at grade crossings. Occasionally, when a jogger or someone walking their dog passed by, I would crouch down on the floor behind the battlements. Usually they did not come up. They would take a lap around the tower, catch their breath, and run back downhill. I liked knowing that whenever I heard a deer give a sudden start, it meant someone was coming.

I cannot remember whether it was up there on the tower, or at school, or at home, but I discovered something new while I was skipping school. My aggression subsided. I lost my anger at the irrational thinking of the people around me. I felt ashamed when I realized that I had only been upset by how other people – people who did not believe in God – dealt with life and death because I myself was so afraid of life's meaninglessness. At this realization, I condemned myself, saying, "You're a self-centered child; you only care about others' worldviews in order to escape your own."

It was winter, and clouds were flying over the tower in dense gray carpets. In front of the tower, a mountain ash bobbed in the wind. Sometimes the little birds perching in it would look right at you, hopping and balancing on the thin branches, eating the berries. When I moved, they'd fan their little wings and flutter as fast as they could.

How long does a sparrow live?

Doesn't matter.

Why are we here?

No one knows.

When it rained or snowed, I would squat inside the tower, at the foot of the spiral staircase. Trampled tissues were strewn on the floor, and it smelled like piss.

What should I do?

Whatever makes you happy in the short time you have on earth.

I don't know what would make me happy. If someone were to ask me what I'd like to do tomorrow – say I'd have all the money in the world, any wish whatsoever, or if a fairy were to land in front of me – I'd run away. I don't know what would make me happy, except to have my father back.

Then you're out of luck, and your life must suck more than everyone else's. Why couldn't you work to make the hungry better off? That would be meaningful, and good.

What's good?

Helping to alleviate suffering.

You could just kill them. Then they wouldn't suffer either.

You can't just kill people.

Why not?

Because everyone has a right to live.

Says who?

People.

How do they know?

They don't know, they just believe so. They think it's rational.

Not all of them. Not Saddam Hussein. Not Goebbels. And why shouldn't what *they* think be just as true?

What is the truth?

I don't know.

There is no truth.

What are we talking about, then?

Silence.

I asked you: What are we talking about? There is no truth? Then why did I ever bother talking about anything? Tell me! Why are you talking to me?

There was no one there.

Esther?

Yes?

Esther?

I said yes!

Esther?

Here, I'm right here!

Esther?

Esther?

Hours, days, weeks. The train tooted and passed in the distance, the joggers came and went, rain dripped from the leaves. The bell chimed at twelve o'clock from the church tower. And then something dropped.

Beauty fell like a dead fly that had been stuck to the window and turned to dust. Good and evil had long since disappeared. Truth? In the fried egg that was my brain, truth did not exist. And reality? Whatever that might be – just one of the thousand realities of this world – well, it had gone off for a swim with its sisters, and my reality was no more real than our dog's reality, or a fruit fly's reality, or a pebble's reality. Reality didn't exist. There were only images, and my interpretations of them, and other interpretations, illusions, and patterns. And that's why I just let my reality splash around alongside all the others, and no longer paid it any heed – I even turned and walked away from the shore where she had left her clothes.

When I wasn't hanging out at the tower, I sat with Grandma on the edge of her big bed, watched her chest rise and fall, and realized that my every thought was nothing but vain, childish noise. What's the point of thinking if there is no truth? It's just mental masturbation.

The therapist I was sent to see, when I was found out after nine months of chronic school-skipping, couldn't help me. He didn't know why the world was here either. There were no pills I could take for all these questions, much less any answers. He should've at least given me a glimmer of hope, a justifiable reason for why my suffering was not in vain. Yes, I was aware that my suffering was small compared to many other people's. But that didn't make it any better. Quite the contrary – it only made it worse.

On the one hand, he tried to reassure me that I could handle all my questions on my own, and on the other, that I would have to make some kind of change, find something else to occupy my mind. I wasn't convinced. So I just said, "I see," and then I didn't say anything more, and neither did he. I looked at the box of Kleenex strategically positioned next to the couch, pulled one out, and stroked it.

"So, you don't know why we're here either," I thought, and I whispered that thought aloud. "In the final analysis, your answers are probably just as disastrous as mine."

He had no reply to that. As a psychologist, he couldn't. Nor was it his job to. Instead, he prescribed autogenic training, which helped me become calm and relaxed, and made my arms feel heavy as lead. But that only treated the symptoms, not the root cause. So I went on suffering, just in a more relaxed way.

Every now and then I'd try to go to a party. I'd take a shower, wash my hair, put on some makeup in front of the mirror, grab the last bottle of perfume Dad had given me, hesitate, put it back, use one of my mother's instead. Then I'd put on my shoes and go into Grandma's room to say goodnight, even though I usually had done so already, and even though it usually woke her up. Then I'd give her something to drink, wipe her mouth, stroke her hair, and caress her forehead, still shiny with moisturizer, since her parchment-like skin couldn't really absorb it. Then I'd go back into the bathroom to wash the greasy moisturizer off my hands, and get this feeling of paralysis: that I wouldn't be able to even leave the house, much less go to a party. So I'd go downstairs, stand in the doorway of the living room, and find Mom lying on the sofa, watching movies in which nobody ever died.

"I was just going to head out."

"Sure," she says, straightening herself a little and smiling. "Just don't stay out too late." Maybe that's just what mothers say, I don't know.

"Well, then I might as well – I mean, I guess I don't even need to go," I shoot back, standing there.

"Oh, c'mon," she chides me. "Esther, what's gotten into you? Go. Just bring my car back in one piece. Have some fun tonight."

"Yeah, well, if you tell me not to stay out too late, it makes me feel that I maybe shouldn't go at all. I mean . . ."

"What's all this about?" she asks, in a cautious tone, as if she's afraid of wrecking something between us, even though she's already looking at a complete wreck.

"Well, what I mean is . . ." I seize the opportunity to pick a fight, maybe because it helps me to leave angry; maybe because it propels me out the door. "What the hell, Mom?!" And I parrot her, mockingly, "Don't stay out too late."

It's embarrassing, but I go on. "What the fuck, Mom? You should be glad I'm going. I can never get away, anyway. I'm always stuck by Grandma's bedside. 'Don't stay out too late.' I never stay out late because I never leave, and now that I'm about to head out, you just have to throw a wrench in my plans. Why won't you leave me alone? Why don't you want me to go? Because I still have a life, and you don't, or what?"

It's absurd and I know it. The only guests who ever visit our house are my mother's, and she's the only one here who makes any dates.

“I’m staying in,” I say finally. “Fuck it all.” The threshold of the front door looms in front of me. It’s not even high, it’s more like just a crack in the floor separating the inside from the outside. Why is this so hard? Why do I feel like I need to muster up so much courage, or figure out the meaning of life, just to take a single step out of the house? Why does it take so much strength? Why does this meaninglessness weigh on me as heavily as a whole ocean? Do I have to hold my breath in order to accrue enough weight of my own, to counterbalance it all and get things moving?

Even my anger has no mass, no weight. It’s like a tiny gust of wind, unable to move the absurd mass anchoring the other side.

“Esther, you know this is all nonsense.” Mom sits up properly and mutes the TV. “Nobody’s saying you should stay in. I just meant that you shouldn’t stay out too late. You know what I mean: just don’t get so hung over that you’re miserable all day tomorrow. I *want* you to go and enjoy your friends.”

I yell, “They’re not my friends! I don’t even know them! They’re just a bunch of fucking children; I don’t know who the fuck they are!” Mom is speechless now. I linger in the doorway a moment longer, hoping she’ll say something that will trigger something in me, give me permission to leave, or else show me that I absolutely can’t leave, because she needs help with Grandma. I turn and slam the door, running upstairs, stomping up the last few steps. “Fuck,” I curse to myself.

“Hello?” It’s Grandma calling from her room. “Hellooo!” I go in.

“Hey there,” I say, “You can’t sleep, Grandma?”

"No," she says. "There's a draft. I think it's coming from the – what do they call it? The little choreographer, that's what she was saying, and if it doesn't rain, that will make a wonderful impression on him." Her quiet babbling relaxes me. I take off my coat, tie my blow-dried hair up into a braid, kick off my heels, hold the sippy cup for her, and stay seated at her side until her hand stops shaking. As her hand calms down, so does mine. Then I flick off the light, and it's dark. Her breath quietly rattles as she sleeps. We're just two stately shadows beside the closet, the desk, the wheelchair, and the bed. After an hour or two – you can never really tell how much time passes when you're in someone's sickroom – it begins to feel as if I'm losing something light and airy. Like my hair is falling out. Like I'm losing something you could just sweep away

15

Maybe it was God holding his breath. Maybe he had deeply exhaled, drawing his chest in to make more room and offer me a new space, somewhere I could move around in freely – free from him, if one can even do such a thing as a human being. I don't know. Something like a vacuum.

In God's silence, to which this world belongs, there is plenty of room for those who do not want him. And if his silence and distance weren't so unbearable, I would write hymns and poems, odes to the silence surrounding him and to his distance, which gives us room to breathe and doesn't compel anyone to do anything. If only it weren't so awful without him, I would build grand temples to this freedom, leaving the center empty, and I'd worship that very emptiness, as a place where there is no need to cower or crawl.

If only it weren't so awful, off in the distance, I would praise God for that space where you're not struck by lightning, where you aren't brought to your knees, where you don't have to die from his presence. I would praise him for all that, if only it weren't so awful.

16

A bare white nave, clearly built in the fifties. The ceilings are high, with lamps hanging from long brown cables. Everything around me is a blur. It's Easter, one year after Dad's death. Not exactly one year to the day, actually, but he died the morning of Easter Sunday. And now it's the morning of Easter Sunday once again, the same exact time, the hour of Dad's death. The congregation is singing "Christ Is Arisen," and I'm fighting the urge to throw up because I'm beyond drunk. Everything around me is spinning. As I exhale through my nose I smell the vodka I was downing all night, until just two hours ago, as I staggered through the woods by our house, all alone.

My brother had come home from boarding school the night before. I was glad to have him home. We hugged in the doorway for a long time, until he let go, a little embarrassed. Then he said that one of our old friends from back when we were scouts had told him that someone was having a cookout today. He wanted to go, and wanted to know if I would come too. I didn't want to at first.

"C'mon, Esther," he said, patting my cheeks with both hands. Then he put his right arm around my shoulders, pulled me in close, and whispered right into my face,

"Your father, my child! Your father would have very much wanted you to go to this cookout with your brother tonight. Come now, kiddo – do it for Dad!" We laughed.

On the way, he cracked open a bottle of beer with his lighter, and we shared it. We walked along the edge of the forest, and the pungent smell of wild garlic growing among the trees prickled our noses. The sun was low. The ground was muddy. Johannes told me stories from boarding school, and kept bursting into laughter while telling me about two of his classmates, who with their overdressed snobbishness and insane opinions actually belonged in jail, we agreed, except that they were so brilliant and so broken, so touchingly childlike and so messed up. I was so glad Johannes was back.

Our old friends were sitting outside a garage about a twenty-minute walk from our house. We got drunk pretty quick. Johannes wanted to head home sometime around one thirty in the morning, and wanted me to go with him. He was tired from the trip. I didn't want to go yet. Slurring a bit, he instructed one of his friends to bring me home later. Before staggering off, he turned around again, "Remember, we're going to Easter Mass with Mom tomorrow morning at six. You can't crash here. Don't forget, okay?"

"Mh-hmm," I said, staying put. I can't even remember why. When I'm drunk, I just don't want it to stop.

One of the guys seated in front of the garage drifted off in his chair, his torso still almost vertical, his chin sinking into the collar of his jacket, still holding a beer bottle in his lap with both hands. I was toying with the tongs, prodding and poking at the ashes on the grill. I don't remember what time it was, or how long I sat there, letting my buzz clear up a little.

Just as I was leaving, the guy in the chair came to and slurred, "Wait, Esther, I'll take you."

I slurred back, "Nah. You sleep. I'm good." And I left, with an open bottle of cheap vodka still in my hand. I hurried across the courtyard in front of the garage, headed along the slightly uphill road, and then took a right, turning into the big black tunnel of trees that formed a huge gateway of sorts, so high that an eighteen-wheeler could've driven through. Although I knew the forest well, and also knew that just a few yards down the road there was a barrier to keep cars out, I still banged my hip right into it in the dark. At first I just leaned there for a while, a little stunned, and then I took another sip. I couldn't decide whether to slide underneath, or climb over it. I was too lazy and drunk for either. Vodka in hand, I groped my way along the barrier, listening to the hollow, scraping sound of the glass against the iron. As I reached the end of the barrier the bottle clinked against the heavy, box-like concrete counterweight. The high-pitched sound tickled my ears, and then everything was quiet. The forest was silent. I walked around the end of the barrier, and after a few yards I took a left, off into the dark forest. I drank some more vodka. I knew there was a trail somewhere out here.

I remember seeing the blurry moon behind the black branches every time I stumbled and looked up. When you drink, your view grows so narrow. And I remember thinking that I could draw those black curtains further down over my eyes – my view was already pretty obscured to the right and left, up and down – and make it even narrower with each sip.

The bottle made a little sound against my lips – *phloop* – each time I took a sip. Otherwise, it was silent. Not an animal stirred, not a single bird startled, no owls called. Not even the whirr of a passing car could be heard up here, although its lights shone on the trees at the forest's edge.

Phloop.

Was I even on the path?

Leaves of wild garlic stuck to my shoes, and slid off again. The tree trunks stayed hidden in the dark – only when you got too close did they rear up, all rigid and proud and in your face. I stopped, held on to a branch, and tapped my feet around, searching for solid ground.

I looked around. The sky was dark. I squinted. The underbrush was black. I listened to the night, took a step, heard a sudden *crack*. Then silence. And then it came: the word "free."

My head was foggy, but I agreed. I swayed, took a sip, paused again. "Free," something whispered, and I nodded, the way drunks nod – not gingerly, as if I were wondering, but simply because my neck couldn't hold my head up anymore. My chin slumped forward, my eyes closed. "Yeah," I thought, and then, with a jerk, my head swung up again, trying to regain its balance, while still reeling. And although I could no longer say whether it came before or during all this, I remember exactly how the feeling came over me. It was something like liberation, like salvation. In some ineffably beautiful way, something ceased mattering. Like it was all the same. I staggered onward, and at one point I fell to my knees. My pants soaked up the moisture from the mud and pressed into my knees like a wet kiss from some big, soft, cold snout. Slimy, rotten leaves stuck to my hands. I had to laugh. I got up again, took a few more steps, and that feeling of redemption spread over me – just like when, all at once, every tense muscle in your body suddenly relaxes at the same time.

"That's it. It's over now." All that inner nagging, all that fighting against my own foolishness – it just melted away. I was finally able to give up the battle over my own headspace, and it was like a deep exhalation that didn't stop. It just kept pouring and pouring out of me. Suddenly I was free of all that Christian clutter, all the humanistic humdrum that forces you to take life seriously and follow made-up rules. I was free of everything I was taught in school, some of which society has agreed upon, and some of which you just follow because you know that, if you don't, you'll be punished. Things society has agreed to without knowing why in the first place. All that talk of dignity – human dignity. Nonsense. Just another superstitious belief. Where exactly is this dignity? Where's mine?

We humans are free because we carry no weight. That's what became clear to me. Nobody can force me to believe that we have innate dignity. Go ahead and tell children all those myths – I don't believe in them. And I don't believe in the inherent worth of this world. It, too, shall pass. Everybody says so.

But it didn't matter what they said, because my "yes" was directed at that absolute fact, not at the theoreticians. And my "yes" had no end. My mouth stayed open, and the air that might have otherwise blown me up flowed with a salutary hiss. My ribs let out a sigh as they relaxed, my diaphragm let go, my legs no longer hurt, my arms weren't heavy anymore, my throat didn't have to hold anything in, and my eyes didn't tear up squinting for an answer.

At some point, the world will be no more. There will be no more consciousness. Dead silence will encompass the universe; there won't be any more inquisitive eyes searching for answers, and there won't be any humans asking for meaning. The stars will quietly orbit one another. No more thoughts to be thought, no more astonishment, no more asking "Why?" Just dead silence. Because there won't be anyone there to keep asking.

And then the cosmos will no longer be called cosmos; the moon will no longer have a name. Darkness is no longer darkness if no eye is waiting for the light. And now we're racing straight toward boredom, the barren wasteland, and death.

Earth and all of humanity, having blossomed like a cactus that only blooms once, will collapse in on itself, and no one will know anything about it.

No eye will have seen it. No moral system will prevail, good and evil will have disappeared, and the universe will be redeemed from moaning and groaning, from breathing and gasping, from whimpering and laughter. From all the noise that was here. There will be silence.

This judgment-free silence – the same silence that will reign when this world is no more – is precisely the silence through which I received this new freedom that night. For those who discover this silence within – those who notice that it has already sunk deep into themselves – this freedom will suddenly unfold and grow, from then until the day when the last human being has died, and the last spirit has been extinguished. And it will continue even after that.

This freedom is joy. It wipes away all tears, because death is no more – only rocks and gases, and suns set on their courses. Those who discover it come to see at long last that there is no need to struggle or strive. They can laugh at the gossip in their villages, their cities, the entire world. They are free of all anxiety about fads, fashions, and supposed authorities, and they have real comfort to offer those who suffer. "This, too, shall pass. Everything passes."

They can close their eyes amid the noise of the present, and the world falls away. Supermarkets topple, hospitals crumble, bombs fall into bottomless pits, friends' calls grow quieter, and children's wishes and old people's prayers and hatred and love are all brought down together. The bonds between brothers and sisters loosen, all worldly worries are let go, and everything grows quieter and smaller and falls farther and farther – deep down, to where no more sounds emerge. Down to where nothing matters. Down into the silence that will one day come for the whole earth.

Those who discover the freedom of this silence within themselves no longer have to fight, and they no longer have to love. Nothingness puts a smile on their faces, the same smile we know from the faces of the dead, from those released from existence. You can attain this sort of smile already here in this life, if only you are aware of the clues, and follow them.

I was free! And so I let things go, and became lighter and lighter, and ran faster and faster and – strangely – more and more happily, through the forest. You don't have to break love's neck to make it stop squawking. You can simply set it down, exposed in the light of the coming downfall of the world, and then you won't hear it anymore. It will become as quiet as the murmur of generations upon generations, and will disappear along with them.

I drank and drank. The curtain closed tighter around my eyes, and I hoped that when I sobered up I'd be able to remember this feeling. I hoped it would stay. No, actually, I can't really describe it. I didn't really care either way. I thought: the way things are *right now* is just how they are. Whether I think about it, whether I remember it or not, whether I believe it or not. This *is* how it is. I'm free.

I lit a cigarette and downed the rest of the vodka. Then I tossed the bottle, heard it hit the ground behind me, and staggered on, bending as I wove under and around the branches. And then, making my way through the last bit of forest, it hit me: Dad. I slowed down and realized, stunned: it's all the same to me – everything, including Dad's death.

At this very moment last year, Mom must have been sitting at his bedside. A year ago right now, she had been by his side, praying.

And yet, it was all the same to me. I didn't care, and that was such a relief. Oh God, was that a relief! It didn't matter; it was all so much dog crap. Fuck the dead. Let 'em all go. Everything will come to an end eventually anyway.

I sighed, happy. Everything was over. It was as if a hammer had fallen.

"Finally," I groaned, drawing the cold air into my lungs, closing my eyes in the dark forest, and exhaling again. "I don't care. I *so* don't care."

Blackout.

17

Somehow I still managed to make my way home that night. Johannes woke me up the following morning. He was horrified I still hadn't gotten up when he came to my room. He must've come by earlier too. I got up, still in the same clothes from the night before. There were leaves in my hair and my boots. I still had everything on. I went downstairs. Mom looked at me and said, "You slept in your clothes? Good Lord, Esther," then grabbed the keys and her coat, and walked out.

There was the traditional Easter bonfire in front of the church, but I have zero memory of it – just as I have zero memory of walking into the church, or whether the candles were lit. But feeling nauseated, trying to focus on the blurred floor tiles between the kneeler and the seat in front of me – all that I remember. I remember trying to hold my nausea back, and freezing. And I remember thinking that just now, this very moment, was the hour of Dad's death, and that all of his friends who were thinking of him last year at this time were here at Mass right now.

I tilt my head back, and suck the air in through my open mouth. I can't stand how the strange, spicy incense sticks to my dry tongue. I stand up with the congregation, but have to sit right back down. Mom and Steffi are sitting two places away, Johannes is right next to me. Are they mourning? I don't know. I can't mourn anymore. The priest, in white, goes from blurry to sharp to blurry again.

I wipe the sweat from my forehead. The congregation kneels. I don't. Not out of protest, but simply because I can't. My head goes from hot to cold, burning and throbbing. I reek. I can't do it anymore.

A year ago I was lying in bed in the attic, in Grandma's cabin, in a white nightgown. Steffi was in bed across from me, also in one of Grandma's old nightgowns. And then I heard footsteps, and a creak on the stairs, but too early. The alarm hadn't gone off yet. Outside, there was snow on the window. These footsteps were coming too early.

It had started snowing overnight. Steffi and I couldn't sleep. We had stared out at the snow until five o'clock in the morning, and then Steffi had gone over to the window, knelt, and said, "If Dad dies tonight, I don't know what I'll do."

And I had said, "But he won't die," and I said my prayer to the good Lord in a soft whisper, "Please . . .thank you," and we had listened as the sound of the brook in front of the cabin grew more and more muffled under the snow.

That was last year.

The footsteps are coming way too early. The alarm hasn't even gone off yet. I keep my eyes closed as the heavy creaking gets closer and closer to our room. There's a soft knock. I squeeze my eyes shut, and stop breathing as the door slowly opens. It's Uncle Hans.

"Kids," he says, "your father . . .your mother just called. We need to go to the clinic." He hesitates. I open my eyes, look at him, then close them again. "She said your father is . . .your father just died." Steffi screams. I turn to the wall.

I hear Steffi's high, stifled voice growing softer and finer, like she's counting heartbeats, or falling drips. "Dad. Dad. Dad."

I get up, go to her bedside, slide under the covers and hug her, whispering, "Don't cry. It's not true, Steffi. Don't cry. It can't be true."

She shoves me from her bed. I stumble backward over the space heater. Suddenly I think of Johannes. How will he handle the news? He can't know about it. Please, don't let anybody tell him. I don't want anything bad to happen. I go over to his room. The door is ajar. He's standing in the middle of the room, his head down, and he's looking at the shirt in his hands, but not putting it on. I touch his hand, and then hold it tight. Without looking up, he takes a small step toward me and rests his forehead on my shoulder. I whisper, "I don't believe it." He shakes his head slowly, and almost flatly says, "Me neither."

That was a year ago, right now. At this exact moment.

It's only been a year.

And I can't take it anymore.

How many more years will it take?

The night in the forest – its message to me – was right on. It doesn't matter. But now the sparkle, the shine of that feeling is gone. It didn't matter, and it still doesn't matter, but I'm still alive, even though it doesn't matter. And I just don't want to do it anymore.

The bells ring for consecration, and the white host is held high.

I want to puke. I want to spew out my life. "Leave me alone," I say to myself, almost pleading. "Leave me alone, just leave me be, I can't stand myself anymore."

And for the first time I experience the despair that comes when you realize that you cannot erase yourself. You have to just endure your own existence. That is your duty, laid on you even though you never asked for it.

That was the consequence of me really believing that after death comes nothing. When you believe that, you don't smile anymore. You don't take it to a talk show. When you believe that, you don't want to convert others. You can't enlighten anyone by saying, "After death, that's it, the end," because you don't even really care about that.

18

"Who are you?"

"Esther."

"Oh yeah?"

"Yeah."

"What's that supposed to mean?"

"I'm me."

"Well, well, well. And who's *me?*"

"Me. A human being. Me. Esther."

"Oh yeah? And what's *that?*"

"Me. I." That's something you can insist on – you can shout it out loud. You can rant and rave, wave your arms, stand up straight, lift your chin, beat your chest, build entire cities, write grand operas, and wave and wave and wave. But it won't really tell you anything.

I gave up trying to win that conversation.

BLACK
AS
EBONY

3

1

Maybe what's most unbearable about this life isn't the circumstances, or the sunrises and sunsets, or all the hours in between, or the almost mute movement of the curtains in the rooms you're trapped in. Maybe what's most unbearable isn't that people say nice things to you, or that you're ashamed of the disconnect between your own suffering and others' obviously worse fates. Maybe what's most unbearable isn't that there are still people who love you and you don't have the strength to make them understand the folly of their ways. Maybe what's most unbearable isn't the cars driving past your house, or the gurgling sound the radiators make, or the twilight blue of evening, and the next night, and the next morning, and the next midday, or the next little movement in the curtain, or the fly on the window. What's most unbearable is probably that there's no real verdict, that the hammer never really falls.

That's why clock pendulums are so horrible, their ticking so terrible – not because it reminds you of decay or transience, but because it is the metronome of indifference. Every second is equal, every distance the same. It's just a beat, with no variation. It's just a beat: not the hammer you're really yearning for, not the starting gun of a race, not the fireworks of a ship setting sail, not the sentence of execution nor the verdict of acquittal.

No, it's just a beat, an eternal beat, a beat granting you no release. It always hits its nadir and just keeps going, and the longer you listen to this metronome the clearer it sounds, the longer and emptier the midpoint becomes as it swings past its nadir and back again. It never halts, never hobbles, and if you close your exhausted eyes in those middle seconds, then its sound wakes you up again, briefly, quickly, just to make sure you know how very strict it is. It has no clear preferences, no propensities, doesn't pull you in one direction or the other. It just wants you to know that nothing is gained, nothing lost, nothing carries any weight, but there's no sleeping here whatsoever, not a moment of rest – and that's why anyone who decides to jump, anyone who willingly leans so far in a horrible direction as to tip, thereby rendering their own verdict, experiences an incredible, if fleeting, sensation of liberation from this beat. The hammer falls, slamming down from above, and the person can finally go this way or that – freed from indecision, the tie over, the standoff at an end.

Such is our longing for justice and judgment. Maybe this is the wellspring of our yearning for God. We want someone to render a verdict – to judge not our enemies, but us. Not just in heaven, but in the here and now – someone who can defend us, and also has the power to judge, so that we don't have to do it ourselves, because we simply can't. It's impossible. I mean, we do it all the time, but our so-called justice isn't just, and our arguments are so very weak.

Maybe that's where our longing comes from. Every human being understands judgment, because we all make judgments every day. Just or unjust, it doesn't matter. We're always rendering verdicts. Perhaps that's because life began that way – with discernment, with the distinction between dark and light, and the judgment that it was good. And because the existence of each one of us began that way: with a "thou shalt." There must have been a moment when we accepted that judgment, because we're here. Maybe once upon a time we said yes, and maybe that's why it's so hard to take it back and nix the verdict we have already issued. Maybe the moment we accepted that judgment was our greatest moment of freedom, and maybe that's why there are no excuses and no apologies. We were probably truly free the moment we uttered that yes, and that's why it's so hard to jump. That's why we find it so binding.

Maybe the will to survive is not a simple, basic urge, but rather a *should*, a *thou shalt*. A brief dialogue with God that we cannot take back – at least not in any clean or tidy way

2

No lightning struck in the years following Dad's death. No voice rumbled forth in thunder. No hot coals burned my tongue, no Christ came to me in a dream, no sea parted, no pillar of fire appeared, and no wind whispered. There was no choir of angels, not even a lone angel, nor was my name called by God. There was nothing. God was silent.

And I will never forget that silence. Today, I sometimes think that there is a power in his silence – a power we cannot even imagine.

When I sat at Grandma's bedside and the closets gawked at me, when the wind bent the branches of the chestnut tree outside but no sound penetrated the glass, when Grandma's breath seemed to confirm the fact that there was nothing else here, and all the objects in the room – the feather bed, the curtains, the desk, and even my skin – seemed to grow heavier and denser, as the nothing grew bigger and bigger around me – God must have conquered it in his own way. It certainly wasn't me. I was no longer fighting. I had lost my name, and with it, reality. Without those things, there is no fight.

And yet, there nevertheless was a victory. If it was silent in those rooms – unbearably silent – God was even more silent. I may have fallen silent within during the years following that night in the forest. At least for several years after that, I remembered only external events, hardly anything internal, and might have fallen silent for good. There were no more questions directed inward, no more hatred whispering within. But God must have been even quieter than all that. His power must lie in this silence. His silence seems implacable compared to the silence of the world. His silence is merciless compared to death. It pushes nothingness to the point of bursting. His battlefield knows no noise, for it is always silence, death, graves, and nothingness. And he didn't head for the underworld brandishing a sword, waving a flag, or shouting – but with closed eyes, a pale mouth, and no heartbeat. God subverts silence. There must be a power there we do not understand.

3

The evening sun was shining through the curtains, and a blackbird was warbling its dreamy singsong from a branch of the chestnut tree in our front yard. About two years had passed since my drunken Easter night in the forest. I was still in school, and still living at home with my mother and grandmother. On this particular evening I was seated beside Grandma's big sickbed, one forearm stretching through the side rail we would pull up each evening so she wouldn't fall out. I would sing old nursery rhymes or folk songs to her – I had the verses down pat because I had been singing them to her every night for three years now. Sometimes her thin voice would rise up, and she would sing along with me. Singing enlivened her. Otherwise she mostly just slept, and babbled a bit of nonsense every now and then. But when I sang with her, she was fully present.

I was holding her hand in mine, like every evening, and it was shaking, just like every evening, though it eventually came to rest. I had been sitting there for almost an hour, mostly silent, lifting the sippy cup to her lips and waiting after each sip for her coughing to stop before lifting the cup back up again. Then I waited for her to cough again, wiped her mouth, adjusted her dentures, and wiped her mouth again.

My eyes wandered around the room for the umpteenth time. It had been Johannes's room when he was little. It had blue-and-white striped wallpaper, a small sink on one wall, an old built-in bed on another wall, and a desk on another. Grandma's sickbed took up half the room. The small nightstand next to my stool was outfitted with disinfectant, an inhaler, a few small green syringes in plastic sleeves, and a pair of disposable gloves. Grandma coughed. I hummed a tune, and then started singing.

She particularly liked the traditional lullaby "Can You Count the Stars?," so I sang it to her every night. But this time something was different. It was as if something was dawning on me, like a new light emanating from each stanza. Something recognizable, something familiar. I continued singing, suddenly wide awake:

> Do you know how many children rise each morning
> with a song,
> free from sadness, care, and worry, singing happily
> all day long?
> God the Lord hears all their voices, in their pretty
> songs rejoices;
> and he knows and loves each one; knows and loves
> you, too, my child.

A strange excitement swept over me. Alert, amazed, my back suddenly ramrod straight, I sat there by her bed, searching, looking for a clue. It was bizarre. My brain and body were fixated on some sensation I couldn't see or even place. It was like that feeling you get when you're trying to remember the name of some actor, just before it pops to mind. It's not even on the tip of your tongue yet, but you know it's there somewhere, buried in your brain. It usually helps to close your eyes – you're certain it's there, and you can almost see it. You fish around for it, but if you get too close it slips away and sinks, until you wait patiently enough for it to surface again and finally grab it.

I kept singing, still distracted by the desire to put a finger on what I was feeling, but the excitement sharpened my attention. I noticed that even though Grandma was almost asleep, she joined in, mumbling along. We got to the end of the final stanza:

> God the Lord, who dwells above us, has bestowed
> his love upon us
> and has not forgotten thee; he has not forgotten thee.

Grandma turned the last few syllables into "Godandthee." That was it. So simple: Godandthee. It gave me a shock: my forearm yanked itself from the side rail, and my hand shot to my mouth. My face was on fire. That was the word I had been looking for. That was my word.

Grandma's mumbling mixed with my strange state of distracted yet heightened attention, and now this word suddenly returned from afar, after eighteen long years – or how long had it been? It appeared like a tiny dot at the end of the street. I want to cry out, "That's crazy!"

I had been looking for this word. Sometime around fifteen or so, I had asked my mother if she could remember it, figuring maybe it was a name? Was it from a song or something? But Mom had no idea what I was talking about. I even asked my siblings, but they couldn't think of it either.

This was my first, my most primal word. Like *hungry, thirsty, tired*. But somehow, I had never understood that it was really two words, not one, and part of a complete thought: "He has not forgotten thee." I had never heard it that way as a child. I had heard "Godandthee," and that sounded serious but also sweet; majestic as the Alps, but also friendly. It went ahead of me as I fell asleep. It was there with me in the dark, behind my closed eyelids, and wouldn't allow me to get lost. It had always stood by, waiting for me here, there, everywhere. And now it had come back to me all at once, like one of those oxygen bubbles that form on an underwater plant, starting out as a silvery fur on the stem, and then suddenly letting go and rising to the surface. That's how it had come back to me – in a rush. I drew my hand from my mouth and laid it on Grandma's forehead.

"Grandma," I whispered. She didn't respond. I leaned over her, stroking her white hair. "Grandma, I found my word again." No reply. "Godandthee," I said into her ear. She was asleep.

I went downstairs to the kitchen, turned on the light, and slid onto the corner bench at the table. Rediscovering my word: it was just like that moment on the shore as a little girl, when I had sat on the warm rocks in front of God. If someone had asked me that evening, "What does your word mean? What is this 'Godandthee' thing?" I would have answered, "It is now. The present."

It had grown dark outside. The blackbird had stopped singing. I lit a cigarette and took a drag, heard the burning tobacco crackle. I saw my reflection in the windowpane: blurred face, propped-up arm, folded hand, and a thin, hastily swirling, rising column of smoke. Godandthee was gone.

4

One morning a few days later, as the trees' black branches began to emerge like silhouettes against the sky, I saw a deer in the garden. It was gently sniffing at a flower bed, its nose burrowing through the blossoms, calmly grazing, undisturbed, in the growing light of dawn. I opened the patio door, expecting it to dart right off, but it merely raised its head and looked at me.

Wind rustled through the crowns of the tall trees and their massive branches.

I stepped out onto the patio. The deer turned its back to me and continued munching. When I clapped my hands to scare it away, it gave a start, a jolt of fear running through its slender limbs, but then stayed put.

"Hey!" I shouted. "Beat it!" and slammed the patio door. The deer ducked a bit and then leapt – one, two jumps – and slowed to an elegant trot. Then it took a few more steps and turned to look back at me, as if maybe it were mistaken. About me. As if it wasn't sure I was actually there.

And I think that was the moment I took hold of myself.

"I" – it seemed to hover somewhere amid the various schizophrenic-sounding descriptions I had read about being human. "I." It couldn't be concocted out of nothing, or reinvented. Nor was it strictly committed to anything. And yet, from somewhere – I have no idea where – "I" emerged, and with it, freedom.

The deer turned back toward the lawn and continued munching.

Perhaps people whose world has been shattered can relate to this better – they know how frightening the white nothingness is that surrounds you when you lose yourself in it. But what I suddenly understood at that moment, and clung to, was that I had seen this nothingness.

"Hey!" I shouted even louder. The deer didn't react. I grabbed a chewed-up tennis ball from the patio floor – our family dog was always bringing things to the patio – and hurled it with all my might in the deer's direction. It landed with a bounce in front of him.

In all the years since Dad's death, I had assumed, with more and more confidence every day, that *there is no such thing as truth*. Meanwhile I hadn't noticed how this phrase gradually grew puffed up and fat, gasping proudly, sweating, and grunting as it went around destroying every other phrase by belittling everything and everyone – myself included. Every insight, every assumption. And yet it had never once looked in the mirror and noticed that it was actually subject to the very same dogma: that if there is no such thing as truth, then it is also *not true* that there is no truth.

And yet, here "I" was. I existed. Reaching for a second ball, I aimed directly at the deer's face. No bullseye, but this time it jumped to the side, pranced around the garden, and then disappeared among the fir trees and into the woods. I was sweating.

"Who are you?"

"Esther."
"Oh, yeah?"
"Yeah."
"What's that supposed to mean?"
"It means *get the fuck off my line.*"

5

Godandthee was a gift. That morning with the deer, four years after my break with God, I reached for it, and, I think, it signaled the beginning of my new faith.

Anyone who starts saying "I" has – whether they want to or not, whether they believe in it or not – ventured into the invisible world. Their "I" includes not just their DNA, not just the imprinting they received in childhood, not just their smile, not just their eyes, not just their skin, but everything underneath all that – everything capable of being loved, pierced through, hidden, or intuited. Their "I" refers to the little bit of freedom we humans might have. The freedom that allows us to bear a name instead of a number.

Those of us who start saying "I" have already ventured into an invisible world, because none of us have any proof of ourselves or our existence. We all secretly, silently rely upon the notion that we are real. When it comes to this unprovable mystery of our own existence, we all appeal to a certain dignity. But it is not visible. It is an assumption – a belief.

And blessed are they who have no conscious formula for it, who possess it without knowing it, who have it even though they hang around on college campuses, or in cafés, or go on talk shows proclaiming the opposite. Blessed are they who flirt with their own existence, saying, "Everything is mere appearance – there is no reality." Blessed are they who can't manage to say anything more about themselves than that they are merely a mass of self-reflective matter. Which ought to mean that we're nothing more than physical beings coming into contact every now and then – merely murmuring dreams, kitschy façades, or well-groomed bits of flesh dressed up in rags we call clothing.

I feel no anger toward people who say things like that, but I hate the underlying spirit of such pronouncements. I'll never forget the scraping and scratching sounds such notions make, because I'm acquainted with the snitch, and I know this is precisely the tactic she uses to whittle things down, to chip away at reality. I can smell that line of reasoning – I can't help but pick up its awful scent – and it makes me want to puke. I'm disgusted by a society that insists upon instilling a sense of self in its children, as if their lives depended on it, only to rob them of it later. "Self? Soul? What's that? We have neither." I lived like that for three years. I didn't just talk about it; it wasn't some theoretical notion – no, it was my direct experience. I lived through it, and I'm lucky it didn't land me in a psychiatric ward.

But then, that was it. I had said "I." And then I began to say "you." And then "my mother," "my sister," and "my brother." And I said "Dad," and knew that it was beautiful.

The old debate still raged on all around me: "There is no such thing as beauty. Beauty is relative, and 'beautiful' is whatever you were raised to think it is. No true statement can ever be made, because there is no such thing as truth; therefore, there is no such thing as beauty." But these arguments no longer threw me for a loop.

How could I prove my love for my father? How could I prove what beauty is – for example, the beauty deep within my mother, my sister, my grandmother, and my brother?

What exactly could I reach for? Where could I direct your focus so you could finally see it? Between their eyes? Above their foreheads? Should I grab a ruler and draw a straight line from my grandmother's white hair, which looks even more resplendent in the bright sunlight, to the branch sticking out of the bush next to her wheelchair, trembling in the wind? Should I grab a compass and draw an arc down to her little feet in their furry slippers as they tap along with the tune my mother has just started singing?

Should I have grabbed a rag and wiped the blush from my brother's face when he said the name of the Iranian girl with whom he had – he was just admitting this to himself – fallen in love? Should I have pressed a damp cloth to his face, let the color seep into it, and then tried to preserve it?

I didn't know, and still don't, how one could ever calculate or quantify any of this. My grandmother, my mother, my sister, my brother – they are simply beautiful, and real, as real as I am. There is simply something about them – you might call it their selves – an instance of freedom that gives them their distinct existence. Somewhere in that I see their reality. I'll admit that when their beauty flashes before my eyes, it first strikes me as mere appearance, but ultimately the power and truth that their beauty contains strike me as infinitely stronger and more solid than any rock.

So if you really must scream, "There is no truth," then you'll have to prove to me the truth of that sentence.

Because even if half the world repeats that same sentence like so many parrots, you'll be hard pressed to find anyone who actually insists that everything they say is really untrue. Nor will you find more than a few who insist that truth is relative when it comes to rape, torture, or cannibalism. They'll be abundantly clear on their views, and even claim to be on the side of truth when they define such things as crimes. They might even dare to say such things are inherently "evil" – above and beyond any cultural, religious, or temporal considerations, and regardless of personal opinion.

I don't know much. I don't claim to know what's good and what's evil. I just have hunches; I don't possess the truth. But I do believe it exists. I believe truth exists above, beyond, beneath, and behind the visible surface of this world, but I also believe it's something you can touch. I believe that things have a "being-ness" – and that there lies the reality of the world, and the truth.

People seek it out. Songs are sung about it, journalists do their best to get at it in the daily paper, and physicists try to calculate it. Sometimes it's missing. Other times it's apprehended in a specific work, squeezed into a three-line verse, or accompanying a piece of music. It could be, say, a sheet of music by Brahms, and here again one doesn't know where to clutch at to get hold of it. Is it between the lines? Between the clef mark and the first bar? Should we pluck at the eighth notes' little tails, or pump our fist at the blaring horns, or memorize the lyrics and recite them daily?

I don't have the truth, but I do believe it exists, and so does everyone else, or we wouldn't bother saying that we wished the world would become a better place. If we didn't believe in truth, we wouldn't bother pronouncing anything unjust.

And so I believe that the truth about this moment exists. Not in our minds, but somewhere. Truth remains true. That is its essence. It is always absolute. It is exalted, beyond our realm of thought. It needs no approval, because it is true; it is here, and it is eternal. Before us. After us. Without us.

I'm thinking all this, and although I'm sure I've heard it all before (I read about truth in philosophy class), I realize that I'm thinking it for myself for the very first time. I'm sitting up in the attic, holding up a stack of index cards I'm reviewing in preparation for my college entrance exams, and I keep dropping them distractedly. A gust of wind blows through the chimney. A thought arises. A fly on the window, and the thought vanishes. I hear a car go by in the distance, and then silence. Another thought, then more silence, then a pause, then another inkling, and then it's quiet again, and then silence expands into the space around me, and at the edge of this silence there's a soft murmur.

Truth. Is. God.

"Lunch is ready," Mom calls up from downstairs.

Truth is God.

I lay my head on the desk.

"Come on down or it'll get cold."

"Truth," I whisper into the wooden grain of the desk, "is God."

"Esther!"

"Shit." I can't get up. I can't answer.

"Esther!"

Truth is God. That is clearer to me than the wood right in front of my face. It's as clear as this lake in the mountains. I'm wading along the shore, and I can see the bottom, white gravel with schools of translucent minnows that scatter with each step. The water is so clear that I can't even see my reflection on the surface. It is utterly transparent, and there is hardly the slightest ripple. I sink my toes into the little pebbles lining the bottom. Above me spreads a clear sky, and the sun is shining, casting a shadow of the fir trees onto the lake.

I lift my head from the desk and just stare. Truth is God. That's all there was and is, and that's everything – before me, before Dad, before humankind; and after us, and even without us.

I'm still slumped over my desk, staring. Finally I get up, go downstairs, through the hallway, and down another flight of stairs into the kitchen. Mom and Grandma are at the table. I sit down. Mom pushes a plate over to me, stands up, and asks, "You'll take it from here?" She goes and gets something to drink. I grab Grandma's fork and, lost in thought, begin to mix the ground beef with the gravy, forming a squishy mound. Then I slide the fork under, and lift it to her mouth.

"Where's my little one?" asks Grandma.

"Here." I shove the food into her mouth.

"She's outside?"

"No. I'm right here."

She turns her face toward me but looks right past me, her gray-white eyes gazing at something beyond. She chews, then pauses.

"That's good."

6

"You can stay, but I'll never get used to you. Sure, I could get used to the fact that you are here. But everything else – I don't know."

I'm in the theater again.

"God?" It's the clown asking – not me. I remain silent.

"God?" It's the clown again. He stifles a laugh. I can't see him, but I know he's lurking behind me, or hanging from the ceiling. He's out there somewhere in this big room.

A few weeks ago, I entered college. A bunch of my fellow students and I were talking, wondering, "Do we believe in God?" We asked each other this. No one did, it turned out. Only two said they could imagine there might be something more to it. We were standing in a circle on campus. I liked that nobody knew anything at all about me.

"What about you?" someone finally asked me.

"I think he might exist, but I don't talk to him."

I don't say that I've been thinking about him nonstop, the entire time, and that I can't think about anything else, and that I'm finding it really hard to go to class every morning and do my coursework. (I guess I'm just doing what I'm expected to do, even though I sense that something much bigger is looming – something outside my own interests, studies, and everything – an approaching "thou shalt" that is far stronger than the dictates of society or university life.) I also don't say that I actually want nothing more than I want God, but have no idea how to access him and don't understand how anyone has the balls to actually talk to him.

"God?" It's the clown again, but speaking with my voice this time, and sounding super whiny. He's hanging way up to the left of the stage, from one of those big black spotlights. He's mocking me, reminding me that I've been there, done that. That melancholy is incompatible with suffering – they cannot coexist – and that melancholy melts away in the face of real pain. The clown always pokes fun at that. He finds grieving funny. Maybe to him, everything is just a kitschy form of melancholy. I myself am revolted when I see other people cry, but I also know I'm preposterous when I myself cry. But, then again, I never do . . .

The other night I cracked opened the Bible again, because I couldn't sleep. I was so restless, all I could do was just lie there and think about God and the past: all the years gone by, all the times I used to speak to him. I let out a sigh. I wanted to read a bit about him. I wanted to read something that had nothing to do with me – thoughts about God from some stranger, someone I didn't know. So I opened the Bible. Immediately I was struck by these words: "You kept my eyes from closing; I was too troubled to speak. I thought about former days, of years long gone by; I remembered my old songs in the night. My heart meditated and my spirit asked, 'Will the Lord reject me forever? Will he never show me his favor again?'"

"Will he never show me his favor again?" It's the clown again. He takes out a handkerchief embroidered with Dad's initials and blows into it, extra loud.

“As if Dad had embroidered handkerchiefs, you idiot,” I say.

“Humans search for meaning.” It’s a new voice joining the conversation, from one of the back rows of the theater. I turn around, and it continues, “That’s why we have to give people something to hold on to.” A small, dim light comes on. It’s at the technician’s console, and I see someone seated there – a bishop? He’s fat, and his face has soft, even overly soft, features.

“Humans . . .” a second voice now chimes in from someone sitting right next to the bishop. This person is also wearing a miter, but, instead of a bishop’s robe, he’s in a T-shirt that reads “Humanism!” “Humans,” he continues, “have more than just a biological side. We must also offer them something that addresses their need for creativity: art, for example. By the way, I’ve brought a little something along with me – here, please, you’re more than welcome to have a taste,” he says as he stands up and opens a little jar. The click of the lid, he says, is proof of its freshness. Biologically, politically, and morally, he says, the whole thing is perfectly fresh. He dips a small spoon into the glass jar as I watch from my spot. “Now, do come give it a try, please.” He holds the little spoon out across the stage, his arm outstretched, and impatiently waves it in the air. The bishop joins him, tries it, and nods.

“Yes, yes,” he says approvingly, “except that it could use a pinch of sense – that’s what’s missing. It just needs a dash more meaning.” He awkwardly pulls a small bag of powder from the pocket of his wide-sleeved red robe, sprinkles a line across the front edge of the stage, tidies it up with his credit card, and snorts it right up – which is rather difficult since he’s so short that he has to stand on tiptoes to reach the edge of the stage. "That's tremendously helpful," he mumbles.

"The main thing is that it's healthy," says yet another voice.

"The main thing is that it tastes good, I always say," retorts the bishop.

"God?" adds the clown.

The conversation about God with my fellow student made me nervous, because it led me to openly express what I secretly believed but had never before said out loud: that he exists. I didn't tell her that my father had died despite my prayers, not even when she said, "How can you believe in God when you see people suffering?" I didn't know what to say to that.

The clown is now at my feet, stretched out on his back and purring like a kitten. The bishop and the other character have disappeared, and the light on the technician's console has gone out. We go on waiting in the darkened hall.

I had been in this theater before, back in high school. It was where I had taken my university entrance exams. After that I'd returned only once, because our grades had been posted; and as I drove off from high school and my adolescence for good, I thought I would never find a way back to God. I figured I would always be fighting him, what with Dad's death and how it tore my world in two. I counted on using his death to storm that silent curtain; I mentally enlisted whole armies, and organized catapults to hurl my rocks at God. But each time, the only thing they would break was my own world – over and over, again and again.

Truth is God, and therefore so implacable that it hurts to push against it. Its sheer density shatters everything, because it's more real than anything else.

Who dares to speak to God? I couldn't. Not anymore. That wasn't a thought; it was something physical.

"God?" It's the clown, once again. He seems to be slowly drifting off in the darkness. I walk along the curtain, toward the exit. A wooden floorboard creaks. Somewhere in the foyer, a door slams. As I reach the corridor behind the main hall of the theater, I pause and listen. There are props gathered there, standing like shadows. I could settle here, it occurs to me. But I could also go back out onto the street and take my life back into my own hands.

"All options are now open to you," everyone told us, as we graduated from high school. That wasn't true, not even in theory, but it doesn't matter. I don't *want* to do just anything. I want – truth. And I don't even know what that really means. Still, I want it. I want it as intensely as a hound who's tasted blood, maybe because I suspect the origin of my existence lies there. No, it goes beyond that, because this ringing "thou shalt" that I keep hearing is quite different from the whispering I heard in the forest, from the vodka-induced purring that said, "You're free." It's as if this "thou shalt" were something that only freedom would jump at – though not the "I-don't-give-a-damn" kind of freedom I experienced in the forest. I do care, and everything matters. "Thou shalt" calls for a certain behavior. And yet: What about my pain? What about Dad's suffering?

Maybe God is a sadist. Maybe, just beyond the border, lies a big baby who had a terrible upbringing and is therefore incapable of taking care of himself. If, as Christians claim, God is love, then it's a kind of love I do not understand. Because it's both far wilder and far more demanding than my own.

Truth, I whisper, is God. I can't move, can't leave this juncture, this notion that has taken hold of me. I stand at this edge, this border; days pass and nights pass. I stand and stand and stand. And then, all of a sudden, comes the moment when I know where I'm standing and realize that for us human beings, there is only one decisive moment in life: the one when we stand before God.

Human life is actually always lived that way – in front of God – and even if trees grow and skyscrapers rise and theories change – even if I pore over my books, finish my studies, get a dog, have kids, and grow old – it all will be happening on this stage, in front of this curtain, even if I can't see it. Old people in nursing homes stare at this curtain every day and cannot escape it anymore. And even if I'm afraid of what's behind it, or that my world could be destroyed all over again, I finally understand that there's nothing else to do in this whole wide world but speak to God – to the spirit that allowed my own to come about.

Why? Because there's truth there. Truth about my life, about my father, about each of us.

No current of air moves the curtain, no footsteps fall behind the black, heavy, densely woven fabric. It's completely dark now. I can't make out a thing. Everything I ever knew is gone. All that's left are the clumps of dust and crumbs on the wooden floor. I kneel. Everything is hushed, except for the steady beat of my existence.

God?

7

The only reason to fear giving your life to God is if you believe you have a better plan. If you believe you know the truth and are clear about why you're here. I don't. I have no choice but to stumble along, following him. Even if it means letting my reality be smashed to bits all over again.

This also means being ready to admit to yourself that you have no idea about how the world turns, about your own life, or about who and what you are, or what you are supposed to be.

Everyone knows how annoying it can be to watch two people conversing. Imagine eavesdropping – let's say one person is a musician through and through, really knows his stuff, and the other is clueless when it comes to music. But instead of just listening, the clueless one doesn't want to set his whole personality aside, or his ego, and so he tosses in a moderately intelligent comment every now and then. Or he asks questions that actually hinder the conversation, since he's only posing them to avoid the feeling that he's just giving up in the face of the genial interlocutor opposite him. So he asserts himself as he can, meaning not exactly as a genius – although who really is a genius? That sort of chit-chat – that kind of debate – is precisely the kind I quit. I could no longer be like that in front of God.

And it was liberating! Just imagine the situation with the musician: the genius exhorting the vapid windbag, verbally storming him, bringing truth into the room, so that the natterer can sit there and finally relate to it – or not. I've done both: recognized the genius as a genius, and stopped nattering.

Even if God didn't roar or storm into my life, the realization that he was God was the loudest thing I'd ever heard. I had to act on it. It was the most powerful thing I'd ever witnessed, even more than all the deaths I'd experienced.

But I only dared turn to him because I ultimately hoped that all those religions – the ones that claim God loves people, and wants to be spoken to – were right. Without that underlying hope, I might not have dared to take that step.

Today, I sometimes long to go back to that time when I turned to God and asked his forgiveness. No, that's not it; it's not the time I long for. It's the place – that plunge downward, that getting to the bottom.

I long for that ground, where all the scepters slip from your hands; where you no longer need to fight for your father's honor because it's now being held safe in a new order not of your own making.

Kneeling there, everything counts, everything matters, but in a wholly different way than you expected. Within such moments of happiness, we are kings – naked kings who have lost their kingdoms. It's like dying, but it's so much more than that, because death can only tear down and destroy; it doesn't have the power to create new worlds. Nor can death create a new order, because it's the great equalizer and has no hierarchy. That's why I consider the rare moments in which existence is suddenly granted a new order – an order that only God can give, whose truthfulness and reality are as concrete and certain as the love I have for my siblings and parents – to be infinitely more powerful than death. They are the moments of greatest clarity in life. You're not thinking of days gone by, nor pondering what's yet to come, because you're living in the present, which is the presence of God.

8

I believe love draws us, pulls us, in – and not only into other people's arms, or through a series of rooms into the outer rooms where our breath fogs up the glass windowpanes. I believe it pulls us much further. I believe love is like a toddler who knows nothing about time – she is insistent, and can only be temporarily, but never quite completely, calmed down. She pulls us toward God, and that's also why we suffer. We feel God's absence and miss him, and it hurts. Not all of us do – I would never try to talk anyone into this idea or put it into someone else's head, or set myself above an atheist. I know there are good reasons not to believe. But sometimes I have the impression that most people are simply sad he's not there, that he's silent. That's often why we, too, sooner or later fall mute.

Back then, I slowly started to speak again. I don't know much, but I am certain that what we say doesn't just stop at the windows. Nor does it just blow away on a gust of wind. It is awaited. Our every emotion, our every movement, is accompanied by this urging, silent, hoping spirit. It's as if it were all about us human beings, as if we had real, great worth, as if what happens here somehow counts, whether we want it to or not.

I pray that he will guide me, that my steps will take me along the path of his truth. I no longer want to distance myself from God.

It wouldn't make any sense.

9

That's exactly how things could have stayed between me and God. I would have thanked him, I would have stood by the sea again and been satisfied by the inkling of eternity we humans experience in rare moments. I would have said "God" when praying, without specifying any further. But things didn't stay that way.

Otherwise, I might have called this part of the book "light gray" as in gray bordering on white.

But I simply don't believe God is merely an abstract, invisible, ethereal thought – a groundless, wavering truth that comes into only tentative contact with the human spirit, if at all. Or that God is a force or notion only interested in purity or clarity or tidiness. I don't believe that, because I'm not from an innocent country.

I wasn't brought into the world by means of a Caesarean section – no, I came in the messy, disturbing, natural way, with tears, sweat, and blood. And as a child I didn't merely admire the poppies in the fields – no, I reached out for them, yanked and uprooted them, held them tight between my hand and the handlebars, and brought them home on my bicycle. And I ate the pigs that were butchered here.

My prayers were never a whisper into a breeze, from my pure little soul to God's pure clarity. They were filled to the brim with dirt, with joy, with underarm sweat and sorrow and garbage and boredom. I don't believe there's some divine spark deep within me just sitting there glimmering amid the darkness, turning toward the great light and praying to be liberated, redeemed, saved from the material world – from everything that can be touched. I *belong* to that concrete reality, that touchable realm.

This insight marked the end of any notion that, when it came to believing, I had to go it alone. I finally understood that my little bird brain wouldn't suffice if I had to come up with a completely new conception of God, and a new way of believing. I couldn't turn myself into a tabula rasa – a blank slate upon which God would need to be formulated anew, from scratch. I couldn't found a private new religion for myself that wouldn't have any blood on its hands – a cool, clean, modern one. I'm not obsessed with purity anyway – that's something for cults, for people who cut themselves off from anything and everything that doesn't fit their ideas.

During the time I turned away from God, I lost touch with reality. With my belief in God, the world came back. And with the world came people, and the stories they had experienced with God.

With these stories came the religions. Every religion that had blood on its hands and didn't deny it seemed trustworthy to me, because I wasn't interested in abstract ideas. I wanted reality – with God. And any time human beings try to deal with the sacred, they are doomed to fail. That's why this very book is full of nonsense and half-baked thoughts. The moment human beings are put in charge of something big, they mess it up. Maybe that's why I'm a Catholic now – I love the story of this religion's founding. Peter gets the ministry from God, and the first thing he does is screw it all up and renounce Jesus, but to this day that story is told. It wasn't just cut out of the Bible. It's part of the consciousness of every confirmed Catholic.

Not that I was even close to any of that back then. I was cultured. I had received a classical, humanist education. I had adopted the conventional anti-Roman Catholic reflexes that, in Germany, practically belong to having good manners.

The only thing that became clear to me as I began reading about religion was that I would never be able to completely shake off the shine or the grime, all the hopes and fears of the generations that came before me – of the eras in which, in Europe, a belief in this one particular God had been grunted in and snorted out, inhaled and exhaled, while asleep and awake, at work and at rest, consciously and unconsciously.

All the thoughts about God in this book already exist elsewhere. All this has been expressed better and more beautifully – and thought out more thoroughly – before.

I understood that at the time. And I readily admitted to myself that it would be ridiculous to think that I could get any further with my own weak mind, and thereby find the truer God. If he wanted to have something to do with us humans – and I had to assume so at that time, otherwise he wouldn't have given us the ability to think about life and death, and to reflect on truth and on him – then I knew that others must know something about him too.

10

***"Ay habibi,"* yells a voice** from the small speakers in the back of the bus as we rumble through the Lebanese countryside. Earlier this afternoon we stood on the Israeli border, but couldn't cross it. We looked from the hills on one side of the fence over into the other, into the same light brown landscape pictured in my old children's Bible. There were little plaques on some of the houses in the zone lining the border. They were green. They marked the homes of martyrs.

I'm here with a church youth group. I don't actually belong to it, but I was allowed to come along anyway because I'm friends with several of the members. We're in the Middle East with an organization that cares for people with physical and mental disabilities, but we have today off.

Potholes rock the bus so much you almost fall off your seat, but Middle Eastern music – flutes tootling alongside wailing stringed instruments and Arabic chanting to the rhythm of the drums – makes the long ride fly by.

The sun is setting. We're driving by the sea, which thunders right up onto the land. There are no gentle beaches here.

Earlier today I took a walk through the most gorgeous cedars. Someone had hung a speaker from one of the ancient trees, and it was playing old flute music. Soon after I passed it, I came across an elderly, little monk sitting on a rock in the hot shade of a tree. He greeted me, smiled, and then in a mixture of English and French said, "You must never be afraid."

"I know," I said.

"God is like the sun," he said, pointing upward, and I couldn't help thinking that it was that same sun that had made the ground here so arid that it was full of cracks. "But," he raised his arm higher, and his index finger emerged from the wide sleeve of his robe as it slid down his arm, "we don't have to be afraid."

"I'm not afraid," I said. He nodded, and smiled at me. I had to grin. Then he laughed. So did I.

I had once asked a Jewish woman to tell me about God, and she had said, "We do not utter his name." I had to grin then, too, just like with this elderly monk, because I understood, and found the attitude of reverence beautiful.

The Muslim God, I once read somewhere, has ninety-nine "beautiful names." There is *al-Haqq*, "the Truth," who represents ultimate reality. I believed in that. There is *ash-Shahid*, "the Witness," who is never absent. I'm thinking of this as the bus bumps along through the balmy night. I spot the lights of Beirut. Dad would have turned seventy today. I will soon be twenty-four. There is *al-Awwal*, "the First," the one with no beginning, and *al-Akhir*, "the Last," the one with no end. I have been praying again for two years now.

As we drive, I can't stop thinking about Israel, about this land that I know only from the Bible. According to Christian teaching, it's where God entered the world as a human being – as a baby. It's also where he was killed – where God's blood was shed.

Rereading the Bible, I rediscover my old anger toward God. And I discover how God responds when someone asks why they have to endure suffering. I can't believe it when I read what he says, because it's exactly what I have experienced. God doesn't give any explanations. He thunders at the inquirer with the sheer force of his being and then, over several pages, goes on to ask, "Where were you when I laid the earth's foundation? Tell me, if you understand. . . .Who shut up the sea behind doors when it burst forth from the womb; when I made the clouds its garment . . .? Have you ever given orders to the morning, or shown the dawn its place . . .?" I weep as I read. I can't believe it. This is the God I've been praying to. This is the same resounding "thou shalt" I heard through all those months before I turned to him.

There are other passages in the Bible where I don't recognize God at all – where he is a total stranger to me. I often skip those pages. I begin to stumble through the Bible as I would through a landscape. The places I can't get through – well, I just can't get through them. Sometimes I run up against them, or just walk away in a huff. When I get to beautiful spots, I linger at length. When I get to strange spots, I hunker down and wait.

At one point, what I found in the Bible were mostly my complaints, my moaning and groaning, and my despair, all reflected back at me. I had little interest in the New Testament. But then, as I began to leaf through it, I found something that suddenly gave me more confidence in the Bible than in any other religious text: the four Gospels. It wasn't the content that astonished me, but rather the fact that they purportedly speak about God's reality as a human being – Jesus.

If I were to start a sect, I mused, I'd orient its members with my own nice, neat version of the basic story. I'd say: this is how it was, and any other accounts are wrong. I'd write a perfectly pared-down gospel, enumerating each part of the propaganda my followers would have to adhere to. But I realized that the Gospels were something else entirely. They told the story of Jesus not just once but four times, one right after the other, each from an extremely different viewpoint, each with its own aesthetic. It was like reading eyewitness statements after an accident.

I appreciated this approach to reality. There wasn't just one version, but four, and on several points they all differed. It was all somehow . . .real. People cautiously feeling their way toward a faith in this Jesus aren't given a flyer with some seven-point plan; instead, they're given a chance to wander through multiple perspectives. They get to circle around this great mystery four times over.

Back in the beat-up bus, as the old Mercedes engine struggles up the switchbacks into the mountains and the lights of Beirut recede far below, I start to realize that God isn't just silent – he doesn't just tentatively lean toward us when our souls respond to him. He isn't there in the room only when people pray for him to descend. He doesn't make his voice audible only when we are waiting or listening for him, or ready to deal with spiritual things. I begin to suspect that maybe he is there with us – has been there right among us – all the time. I slide the small window wide open and wedge the smelly orange wool curtain behind my headrest so it doesn't blow in my face. The warm scent of herbs and bushes that have basked all day in the blazing sun mingles with the diesel fumes. Crickets all but drown out the hum of the engine. It's gotten dark, but it's still warm.

Godandthee. The sea. All the sunrises of my life. All the mornings with a fresh blanket of snow. All the free, mysterious moments of grace, in all the varied ways I've experienced it – all those tender caresses from God – they aren't mere sounds in a noisy world, I think, nor some kind of song running through the universe, nor the magic that sophisticated souls describe experiencing in moments of bliss. They aren't some whispers borne on a spring breeze, nor delicate heavenly murmurs. No, the Word was made flesh. Maybe. Who knows what to say to all that? All you can do is get down on your knees before it.

Someone has turned the music up again. It sounds like Arabic disco, replete with strings and keyboards. I light a cigarette. I'm sitting at the very back of the bus, next to the priest who's come along with our group. "Smoke?" I ask, offering him one. He nods and pulls one from the pack. I look at him, assuming he's one of those uptight do-gooders who insist on the importance of going to church only because they have no friends. He's just finished his doctoral thesis, "Ulysses on the Cross: The Christian's Relationship to the World."

"I thought Catholics didn't have any relationship to the world," I say, which makes him laugh.

"I'm afraid that's a bunch of bull," he replies, and now I have to laugh.

Back then, the only thing I liked about the Catholic Church was that it involved kneeling. At the time, I actually knew almost nothing about the church, except, of course, that it was anti-body and anti-woman and all the rest – in other words, I knew all the things a postmodern European education teaches you.

I carefully flick the ashes out the window, then tap the priest on the shoulder.

"Tell me about your thesis," I say.

"What?" He squints, tilts his head, and puts his hand to his ear, because he can't hear me over the loud music.

"Tell me about your thesis. About Ulysses on the cross." And he does. He tells me, in detail, about his entire dissertation. It's a relentless onslaught of new ideas, and it takes a few hours.

Afterward, I could've jumped for joy: to me, every last word had been a new revelation. Nothing cheesy; no hippy-dippy Jesus with a circle of crazy robed friends. Instead, one philosophical insight after another, offering me a completely new view on just about everything.

There are beautiful, crazy, overwhelming sides to every religion, but none goes as gaga as Christianity. In no other religion does faith entail such lofty claims, or demand as much as it does of Christians, whose God supposedly ended up on a cross. As all this becomes clear to me during our conversation – the theology surrounding it, the philosophy behind it – its truth is so far-reaching that it seems to point to another country, a foreign land, a wholly new world. And yet, at the same time, it seems so simple. It seems to be something about love. Something astonishing; something grounded in a deep affection. I don't really know what it is, but I'd like to find out.

11

"Esther?"

"Yeah." I was still asleep, lying in bed in a hotel room, when my phone rang from under my pillow.

"Hey – did I wake you up?" It's Johannes.

"Nah, you didn't, I was almost awake." I lie on my back, eyes still closed, and set the phone on the pillow next to my ear.

"I don't want to bother you," Johannes says, "I can call back later." His voice is odd – strangely low and halting.

"Johannes?"

"Yeah?"

"Were you at the doctor?"

No reply.

"Johannes?"

He doesn't answer, but I can hear him breathing, so I repeat my question. Same result: evasion.

"Esther, if you're still groggy, I can call back later," he says, as if one of us weren't all there. I swing my legs out of bed and sit up, both feet on the floor.

"Johannes, what did the doctor say?" I ask, pressing my hand to my forehead. A high-pitched whine has begun behind it, like a bunch of little dentist drills.

"The fucker's malignant," Johannes yells, bursting into tears, if you can even use the word *crying* for the sounds coming through the earpiece. I get up and pace from one corner of the room to the other, pressing the receiver to my ear and gulping air into my lungs as if that might be able to calm my panic.

"Johannes, this is different than Dad's," I say, trembling. "Besides, God . . .God has commanded his angels to guard you, so that you will not strike your foot against a stone. Listen. This is different than Dad's. We have nothing to fear, Joh."

"Okay," he concedes, exhausted.

"Where are you? Have you talked to Mom yet?"

"I'm going over today. She's at the cabin. It's only an hour away."

"Good, then I'll tell Steffi, okay? I'm attending a seminar in Berlin, and she lives just around the corner from here. We're all in this together. None of us is alone. You got that? We're going to be taken care of. You don't have to be afraid. So what are the doctors going to do next?"

"I dunno. Schedule surgery. They've got to cut the thing out. I googled it, Esther. It looks pretty grim."

"What is it?"

"A malignant melanoma." His fear is so audible that it makes me sick.

"They're checking to see if it's gotten to my lymph nodes yet."

"Johannes?"

"Yeah?"

"You know what? I'm not afraid of this fucker, and you shouldn't be either. Don't let it mess with you. You belong to God, and he's bigger than any bullshit tumor."

"Yeah."

"I love you, Joh."

"Love you too."

We hang up.

I kneel beside the bed.

12

Before they operated on him, they warned us that his face might be permanently disfigured, since the melanoma was right on his temple. Mom, Steffi, and I watched as he was pushed away to the operating room on a gurney, and then Mom, Steffi, and I went to church. We prayed. After an hour or so, Mom and Steffi went for coffee. I stayed put. I couldn't be anywhere but there, in front of God. I told him I wanted my brother whole – no shoddy compromises, no drooping eye, no drooling mouth.

"I want him as beautiful as you made him, God. You're *God!* Direct the doctor's hands, bless his fingers, don't let anything guide the knife other than your power; remove everything that could harm Johannes. I'm his sister. I believe in you. I'm giving you my unconditional trust, just please keep him safe and sound and whole."

Three hours went by. I prayed, grew silent, prayed again, and tried to persuade him. I begged and howled. I went from calm to fearful and back again. I mustered up all my courage and was brave, then lost it and fell helpless again. All the while, I stayed with God. Until his light dawned.

And I kept on praying as daybreak came, bringing the greatest grace I have ever known – a morning when, all at once, my stammering was interrupted and everything in my entire being brought forth the answer: You are

God! And with that recognition came the realization that I didn't have to do anything at all, because God's love for Johannes was so much greater, stronger, and truer than mine.

13

It was one of those balmy nights that make summer so sweet. Johannes and I were at a pub, seated outside, and he was looking handsome again: the stitch running from his ear down to his lower jaw had healed well, his hair had grown back, and girls were eyeing him as they had before, their hearts visibly melting. Music wafted from the open windows behind us. One of Johannes's best friends put down two beers in front of us and announced that he had to go back inside because there was this insanely hot waitress at the bar – oh God, was she ever cute, and it seemed like she was totally into him, so hopefully . . .He disappeared. We laughed. "If a girl comes running out screaming, I guess we'll know why," Johannes said.

I was happy, even though it was an unfamiliar town: we had only come because Johannes had another appointment here tomorrow. Things had been fairly calm since his first surgery. It had gone well, and they had removed everything. I had made the whole family come to church with me, and we had sung the old hymn, "Praise to the Lord, the Almighty."

When we got to the verse that talks about God being our health and salvation – about how he shelters us beneath his wings, gives us everything we need, and ordains everything so graciously – we all choked up. Our voices wouldn't make a sound. Because even if we knew it was true, we couldn't say it out loud. Life can be such a paradox, and faith equally paradoxical. I felt as if I were standing in front of two towering cliffs, and that tears were the only thing that would be able to find a way through the gap between them.

After that, things were calm for several months. Johannes and I talked a lot on the phone – almost every other day. I'd call him on my walk home from campus, and we'd catch up on all the good stuff or the nonsense, depending on how the day had been. One night I woke up and realized I'd been murmuring the Lord's Prayer in my sleep.

In the dream, I was standing by the whitewashed corner wall of a familiar-looking room. I went around the corner, and there stood Johannes. His head was tilted downward – he was looking at his hands – but then he raised his eyes to look at me, and in his eyes I read, "There's no God. We're lost." It was the most terrible, hopeless thing I had ever seen or felt – far scarier than what I had experienced in church on the first anniversary of Dad's death. It was so much colder and revolting.

I froze at first, but then said, "Johannes, come, you need to pray. Now." I walked over to him, grabbed his arm, and pulled him to his knees, down onto the concrete. And then I started stammering the Lord's Prayer, which woke me up. I was lying in bed, befuddled, my heart racing. I was unbelievably afraid. I finished praying, and then lay there, motionless, sweating.

"God?" I whispered. "Why does it have to be this way?" Light from a streetlamp fell through the shutters, casting streaks on the floor. No answer. "God, are you even there?" Silence. I had done everything I was supposed to. I just couldn't understand. I went back to sleep.

Two days later, Johannes called to say he was at the doctor's. They had found a new lump, he said. On his face again. He asked if I could go in with him for the surgery, and if I could tell Mom and Steffi.

This was why Johannes and I had met up here in this town. First we'd gone to a big bar with his friend and had Long Island iced teas. A flamenco combo was playing music we had grown up with – we'd gone to Spain so often as kids that we'd grown up dancing to it. We traded memories and laughed a lot. We got hilariously drunk, and at some point we ended up sitting out on the sidewalk in front of this other pub, the one where Johannes's friend had a crush on the waitress.

"Do you pray? Like actually pray?" I asked Johannes. His friend was still inside.

He leaned back.

"I don't know. Not like you, I guess."

"Mm-hmm."

"I guess my relationship with God is different than yours. Like this is something I have to do on my own, you know? I think he wants us to tackle things for ourselves. I don't believe he intervenes in human affairs. I don't know . . ."

"So, he's just sitting like some fat cat up in heaven, just watching, or what?"

"I dunno."

"I don't want to bug you, really, but I do think that if you deny that God can do anything, then you're denying his greatness, you know?"

"Let's not talk about it. I know your beliefs are different than mine, but I need to conserve my strength right now. Positive thinking – that's what the doctor recommended."

That's not enough, I thought. I didn't say it, but he knew that's what I was thinking.

"You can pray for me," he said, looking at me a little sheepishly.

"Right," I said. I looked up at the sky, pretending to be huffy.

We laughed.

Later, as we lay on the guest couch in the house where we were staying, I realized that, just as a sunrise or a musical overture or a morning with a fresh blanket of snow can unfold the divine, the divine will that took on human form can also reveal itself in other humans – in this case, my brother Johannes.

He was asleep now. As he was falling asleep, he had grabbed my hand. I held it tightly, just as I had at childhood birthday parties where you don't really know the other kids. Just as I had at Christmas, when Johannes had gotten a robot and was standing next to me, holding my hand, and I said "Wow!" for him because he was too excited to speak. Just as I had when we jumped off the rocky outcrop and down into the ocean, when we were still half kids and only half teenagers. Just as I had when we had prayed for Dad to get better.

Thinking back on it now, I feel the urge to get up, go to my room, and scream into my pillow. But back in that dark room on the guest couch, the only thing I felt was gratitude. I just lay there, in the presence of the love from which we had come, and through which we were related, even before we were born. That love was present in the room, and not just in a limited, time-bound way, but as a divine power which still touches me today, which is why I can't just jump up and run to my room and scream. The only thing I can do is stay put, speechless. I have no words for what Johannes means to me, much less for the one who made us siblings and gave us life.

In the hospital the next day, we had to hold on to the railing and pull ourselves up the stairs. We were still pretty loaded, and laughing, knowing that the doctor would smell the residual alcohol on our breath.

"You two are impossible," Mom said. She probably would've laughed along with us had she not been so scared. "Pull yourselves together, would you?"

Back in the stairwell, Johannes had actually been laughing so hard that at one point he'd even sunk down onto one of the landings. Knowing it wasn't appropriate to laugh didn't make it any easier not to. But by the time we left the examination room, we were no longer laughing. And we couldn't, for weeks and weeks afterward. The oncologist said they'd have to operate on Johannes again – basically, half his face might have to be cut away. Mom and Steffi went pale and sank backward against the cabinet, and all the color drained from Johannes's face too.

God is terrible. As beautiful as he is – as infinitely deep as his love and affection for people may be – I am terrified of him. And the terrors that overcame me back then still hobble my prayers. And it's a lie when certain congregations claim their message has nothing to do with threats or condemnation, but is only one of celebration and affirmation. It's not true. It simply isn't the case.

God allowed himself to be put to death on a cross here in this world. That's one of the cruelest ways to die. God allows people to be scared to death. People like my brother. God said everyone in this world should take up his or her cross and follow him. No one ever said it would be funny. No one ever said the world would be our oyster.

No, our faith, the Christian faith, has a touch of terror to it. Our faith goes "Boo!" Our faith is fully aware of how nasty the world is, and of how much terror lurks in it. Only then, after recognizing that, do we get the good news, the message of affirmation. Without that terror, there'd be no reason whatsoever to stand in the pulpit, beaming like an idiot, and addressing people who are in real need – people whose marriages are falling apart, whose children are ailing, whose siblings are dying, whose parents are slipping into dementia, whose hearts are breaking, or whose dignity is being violated – and lulling them to sleep with a bunch of cozy blandishments and kitschy social commentary.

God is terrible. God roars. God stays silent. God seems absent. And God loves with radical ferocity. The moment he assumed a human form, entering this world in the flesh, he brought with him the massacre of the innocents. That's how God came into the world. His appearance in human history might have made Mary smile, but that wasn't the only time he appeared, and smiles weren't the only reaction. His entrance sparked a drama. He must have known it would. Our redemption, all the entanglements between us and God, our history of guilt, our distance from him – all of it is probably worse, more complicated, and much more serious than we might believe.

I don't understand God. I tell him as much, too. And I tell him that his standards are too high. That we're too small for him. That he can't make such strict demands of us. If his will weren't the very reason for our existence, I would question him, all day, every day. Because it would imply that perhaps we are actually taller, stronger, and greater than we pretend to be – or even want to be. But what do we know? Who of us created ourselves?

14

Three months, they said. Johannes was twenty-three when his disease was discovered, and when he heard he had three more months to live. The cancer had spread to all his organs, so after delivering that news, they simply sent him home.

"There's nothing more we can do. We're so sorry."

A few days later, we were seated around the table at home for lunch. No one spoke. Our old silver spoons clinked against our soup bowls. Johannes moaned. It hurt him to swallow, because the radiation had burned his throat, both inside and out.

"Human beings aren't made for this," he said, suddenly. He had stopped eating, but his spoon was still in hand, and he was staring at his bowl. Tears were running down his cheeks. "People aren't made for this."

Mom, my uncle, and I stopped eating.

"Nobody can possibly handle this." Now he was staring blankly ahead, looking almost astonished, as if this thought had struck him with a crystalline sharpness and become completely clear to him. Tear after tear rolled down his cheeks, and fell into his bowl. "To know you're going to die . . .we're just not made for this. No human being could ever handle it." He slammed his spoon down and shot to his feet. The soup spilled. I thought I was going to puke. All the color vanished from my mother's face. She went white, and my uncle did too. One door slammed, and then a second, and then we heard screams from the basement. Mom gripped the arms of her chair with both hands, her shoulders pushed up tight, her face grim, as if under pressure – as if someone were crushing her eyeballs.

Then I heard a windowpane shattering in the basement, and jumped up and ran downstairs, half shouting, half whispering, "Oh God! Help us, God!" My knees were shaking.

"God!" It was Johannes's voice, cracking. "God!" I heard him yell again from the laundry room. "How loud do I have to shout for you to hear me? What do I need to scream in order for you to finally hear me?"

I turned the corner at the boiler room, and there, in front of the whitewashed wall, stood Johannes. He looked at his hand, which was bleeding, and up at me. I saw hell in his eyes. It was as if he were saying to me, "There is no God. All is lost." I was horrified. I grabbed his arm. "Johannes, you need to pray. Now." I pulled him to his knees, there in the middle of the concrete floor, where it dipped down toward the drain. I closed my eyes.

"The Lord is my shepherd; I shall not want. Though I walk in darkness, no harm will befall me, for you are with me. You protect me, O God; you are my only king. Help us wretched ones, for we have no other savior but you, and trouble lies before our eyes. Father . . ." I was trembling so badly, my voice broke.

"Father." Johannes knelt before me, his head bowed so low I could see the nape of his neck. "Our Father, who art in heaven, hallowed be thy name," I continued, though I could hardly speak. "Thy kingdom come, thy will be done, on earth as it is in heaven." Johannes remained silent. "Give us this day our daily bread, and forgive us our trespasses, as we forgive those who trespass against us. And lead us not into temptation, but deliver us from evil. For thine is the kingdom, and the power, and the glory, for ever and ever. Amen." I didn't wake up afterward – this wasn't a dream.

I looked around. We were kneeling on a gray concrete floor, next to the drain, and it was freezing cold. Then, a soft "Amen" from Johannes. He looked exhausted. I felt ashamed of having forced him to his knees.

We went back upstairs. Mom was still sitting in her chair, as pale as before. I couldn't read her face, because I didn't even recognize it. Our uncle was shouting.

"Good job!" he cried out. He was earnest. "That was very good, Johannes. Somebody had to say it. You did. You did the right thing."

"But the windows . . ." Johannes said, "I've destroyed them."

"Yeah. It's all good. You're going to be okay." Our uncle smiled, and somehow that day passed without any further insanity.

15

I don't want to say all that much about my brother, because that's his story with God. I don't need to interpret it. I only know one thing, and I'm not the only one – my mother and my sister also experienced it. From that day forward, Johannes grew so quickly in his faith that none of us could comprehend it. A friend later told me that when he asked Johannes where it had come from, he told him about that moment in the basement when he'd yelled at God and then prayed. All of a sudden, he said, God was just there. He couldn't mount any defense; there was no resisting it. But I didn't know any of this at the time.

Johannes was often silent for days on end, and when I couldn't take it any longer, and started to cry, and told him that I couldn't stand not knowing how he was doing, since he was always so quiet, he said to me, "I'm fine, Esther. I just need time. I'm actually praying – all the time."

Sometimes he'd cry out in pain and I'd panic, thinking I might be losing my own faith, but then I'd hear him pray in a way I can't even begin to explain, and that's when I realized that I hadn't understood a thing up till then. I had grasped that God was far vaster than all my hopes and dreams, and deeper than anything I could ever possibly say about him, but I had no idea how close God could come to someone in need of him.

And it was in those moments, when pain pounced on my brother and racked him, that I began to thank God for having allowed people to torture *him*, and that he – God himself – had cried out in agony. If it hadn't been for that, I wouldn't have been able to talk to him. I might have politely continued to believe in him somehow, but I would also have thought, "Come on down from heaven first. Suffer first, before you ask us to believe."

I could no longer say that, because God had already suffered. And, based on the way Johannes spoke to him, it seemed as if he were suffering all over again, right now, with Johannes – it seemed that he wouldn't move an inch from this child whom he loved, or let him out of his sight for a second. It seemed as if he'd been promising, all along, not to resolve his own sufferings or put them to rest even one second sooner than the sufferings of this young man lying in bed. He stayed and stayed. Meanwhile, Johannes would turn his face and look at him. I saw all of this. I was there for all of it, and I am a witness.

And yet I have no words to describe those moments, those encounters. This was my own brother; this was Johannes, and the idea that he could die, and that one of the three months the doctor had given him was already gone, was more unbearable than you can imagine. Sometimes it felt like my soul would squeal like a stuck pig, with every second bringing me closer to the day when my little brother's body would be washed, when his chest would cave in under his tuxedo, when we'd tuck flowers into his pale white hands and the casket would be carried out.

When Johannes could no longer walk up the stairs, we set up a bed for him in the den. I slept in the room next door, on the living room sofa, separated only by a curtain.

Fall turned to winter. One afternoon I ran out onto our patio and right into the snow. I couldn't bottle up my feelings any longer. I said to God, "Stop messing with me. I can't handle it anymore. I'm losing my faith; and if you let Johannes die, I'll lose it completely. I know you're there. Really. Do as you will: I'm not threatening you. I'm here to serve you; I belong to you, and so does Johannes. But it's just a fact: I *know* I'll lose my faith if Johannes dies. It's more than I can handle. Not Johannes. Please. Not my brother. You can take everything else from me. Take my faith, tear my world apart. But don't take Johannes."

And what happened in response to all this was that my faith grew. I had nothing to do with it. It didn't belong to me anymore. But starting that afternoon, it just returned of its own accord, and grew and grew. Ever since, I have not been able to say why I believe in God. Believing is not an act of my own doing.

Johannes was given a similar faith. One time I went to him and cried, saying I was afraid that he was going to die. He took my hand, smiled at me, and said, "Don't be afraid, Esther. Just believe. That's all."

"I love you," I cried.

"I love you too," he said, "You know I do."

What I didn't know was where his sudden faith came from. It wasn't like he was fearfully clutching at straws. This was cancer – this was life and death – and in a situation like that, straws don't hold. I knew my brother. But this strange, deep faith that he radiated all at once – the earnestness of his prayers, the clarity of his gaze, his sheer beauty, his matter-of-factness before God, his maturity, and his calmness – all this was new, although in the end I also suspect it was simply a new expression of what had always been there.

In other words, he was completely there, and his whole being responded to whoever was in front of him. You no longer needed a loving gaze to be able to really see him. I had always loved Johannes. But the flame that love sparks was no longer just a brief flicker, a momentary, passing thing. It was now present and visible all the time. Love was there even in the silent gaps between our words and conversations: a simple, constant chord underlying it all – a love that said, "I'm here," and took away all fear.

Christmas was coming. It snowed. The city grew quieter. It snowed more – so much that the power went out. Johannes, Mom, Steffi, and I waited. We lit candles, we prayed, and when we stopped praying, God stayed with us, in every room. Never in my life had I experienced such a deep, fundamental reality as I did then. It had never been so concrete, so dense, and I had never before experienced such redemption as I did when the storm was raging outside, and we sat together quietly, and felt we had survived something. We didn't know what the end would look like, but we knew it would not be filled with terror, and each of us had a surprised look on our faces – a sense of amazement.

Anyone who has felt the presence of God so deeply – on the rough ground, where it's hard to lie, and where fear, like a thousand pill bugs, looks for little holes through which it can enter you and bore farther – anyone who has lived in the ring of fire God can light up around you, casting out any other power, has no more words for God. For them, God is just real, more real than any rock.

They no longer bother debating God's existence, because doing so would seem too absurd.

Johannes was often in pain. He didn't take morphine, and he didn't doze off. His various pain blockers worked only moderately well. His agony was very real. The rooms we inhabited didn't take on a rosy glow, and he didn't get a halo. But what we all experienced – and this is the only way I can explain why, at a certain point, we stopped praying for a miracle and just prayed for God's will – was that the order of our everyday world was permanently suspended. Meanwhile, we perceived how the cancer also fought for its right to be seen and heard, how it wanted to lay claim to its own reality, and to be heeded.

Understandably, our friends kept fighting to preserve the order of their everyday world. They'd come by to comfort us, to encourage Johannes to keep up the fight, to cheer him up a bit, to bring him back into the world they had shared, and to tell stories – for example, to convince themselves that he was doing okay, and still healthy – but they now found themselves in an upside-down world, one where Johannes was comforting them. He told them that, instead of chatting, he'd prefer to pray, and that they didn't need to be afraid.

The order of the world had been changed. The new one, given by God, had a hierarchy in which Johannes's cancer was at the very bottom. The cancer screamed and howled so much that at one point my brother said to it, "You can leave. I've learned all my lessons. Just go away now."

Within this new hierarchy our desires, wishes, and will were still clearly there, and still counted, but all of a sudden we didn't hold them in such high esteem as we had before. We were kings in those moments – in those hours and days of happiness that stretched from breakfast to supper and on into the night – naked kings who had lost their kingdoms.

"Nothing but God," I wrote in my diary.

And so we didn't think or pray ourselves up into heaven. Instead, we suffered and rejoiced and loved. Here. In the present.

16

"Johannes?" He's beaming at me, standing beside the couch in the living room where I'm lying. "Huh? Why are you grinning like that? You got a date or something?" I ask.

"You wanted something from me."

"Oh, yeah!" I say. "That's right! I told you about that fight I had yesterday. I've thought it over, and I just feel so stupid. I don't know. I don't need to fight. It's enough that I'm Esther. I'm Dad and Mom's daughter, I'm Steffi's sister, and yours. I'm a child of God. Yeah, I can be a little crazy at times, but I know who I am, and I'm not going to let anyone grind me down, as if everything about me were entirely wrong."

He smiles. He seems a bit fidgety.

"Do you get it?" I ask him. "Anyway, I think I'm pretty good. At least not a total idiot."

He laughs. "Esther, I know that."

I sit up. "I just wanted to tell you."

"I know."

"I love you."

"I know."

We grin.

"Esther?" He turns around for a moment, looks at me, and raises his eyebrows.

"Hmm?"

"I have to go now."

"Okay. Go."

He beams at me.

I turn over and go back to sleep. Early in the morning I wake up again. I have no idea what time it is. I get up, still groggy, and open the curtain to the den.

"Johannes?" His body is lying there, relaxed. "Johannes!"

He's gone.

Other Titles from Plough

Love in the Void: Where God Finds Us
Simone Weil
The great mystic and philosopher for our age shows where anyone can find God.

Escape Routes: For People Who Feel Trapped in Life's Hells
Johann Christoph Arnold
Using real-life stories, Arnold maps the way out of loneliness, frustration, alienation, and despair.

Everyone Belongs To God: Discovering the Hidden Christ
Christoph Fredrich Blumhardt
Do we have to make everyone on the planet into Christians?

Perfectly Human: Nine Months with Cerian
Sarah C. Williams
They only had a few fleeting months together, but in that time Sarah's unborn daughter would transform her understanding of beauty, worth, and the gift of life.

Plough Publishing House
845-572-3455 • info@plough.com • **www.plough.com**

151 Bowne Drive, PO Box 398, Walden, NY 12586, USA
Robertsbridge, East Sussex TN32 5DR, UK
4188 Gwydir Highway, Elsmore, NSW 2360, Australia